Advance Praise for Still Friends

"After forty years of psychiatric practice, I have concluded that there is only one psychological problem: the inability to succeed in close relationships. Barbara Quick, in this well-written, insightful book, examines two of our closest relationships, marriage, the least successful, and friendship, the most successful. While there are many reasons marriages fail, the most common is trying to make-over your partner, something we never do with out best friends. We always accept our friends the way they are. If we didn't, we'd soon lose them. Divorced couples, who now are able to accept their partners as they are, may find they start to recapture many of the reasons they once cared for each other, even, at times, sexual interest. If you are divorced, read this book and you will learn the value of making friends with your ex. If you are still in a troubled marriage, treat your partner as a friend and you may save your marriage."

WILLIAM GLASSER, M.D., author of *Getting Together and Staying Together/Solving the Mystery of Marriage* and *Reality Therapy.*

"This book is a beacon, beautifully and movingly written, that illuminates the way for ex-partners who wish to preserve some m░░░░░░ ░░ ░░░░
and friendship."

MATTHEW MCKAY, PH.

"When parents can remain friends as the couples in this book have done, it helps the children adjust to their new lifestyle. The effect of discord in the home often makes children feel as if they are at fault for the breakup of their parents' marriage. This excellent book deals with this very important issue and gives those children a better chance at becoming successful in their own lives."

JUDYE FOY, International Vice President, Parents Without Partners, Inc.

Still Friends

Also by Barbara Quick

Northern Edge: A Novel of Survival in Alaska's Arctic

Still Friends

*Living Happily Ever After...Even If Your
Marriage Falls Apart*

Barbara Quick

WILDCAT CANYON PRESS
A Division of Circulus Publishing Group, Inc.
Berkeley, California

Still Friends: Living Happily Ever After . . . Even If Your Marriage Falls Apart
Copyright © 1999 by Barbara Quick

All Rights Reserved under International and Pan-American Copyright Conventions. Published in the United States by Wildcat Canyon Press, a division of Circulus Publishing Group, Inc. No part of this book may be reproduced in whole or in part without written permission from the publisher, except by a reviewer who may quote brief passages in a review; nor may any part of this book be reproduced, stored in a retrieval system, or transmitted in any form or by any means electronic, mechanical, photocopying, recording, or other, without written permission from the publisher.

Editorial Director: Roy M. Carlisle
Copyeditor: Jean Blomquist
Cover Design: Eleanor Reagh
Interior Design: Candace Bieneman & Margaret Copeland
Typesetting: Margaret Copeland—Terragraphics
Typographic Specifications: Body text set in 11.65 pt Bembo. Heads set in Bembo Bold

Printed in the United States of America

Cataloging-in-Publication Data
Quick, Barbara.
    Still friends : living happily ever after . . . even if your marriage falls apart / Barbara Quick.
        p. cm.
    ISBN 1-885171-36-6 (alk. paper)
    1. Divorced people—Psychology. 2. Divorced people—Family relationships. 3. Interpersonal relations. 4. Friendship. I. Title.
HQ814.Q53   1999
306.89—dc21   99-38533
                                                        CIP

Distributed to the trade by Publishers Group West
10 9 8 7 6 5 4 3 2 1   99 00 01 02 03 04

For John, once again,
with joy and gratitude
that we're still friends,

and for Julian,
the child we adore and proof
that love always has its reasons.

Author's Note

To protect privacy I have disguised certain characteristics as long as those aspects were not important to the central issues being discussed. These aspects may include names and circumstances.

Contents

Introduction

There's no doubt that the decision to end a marriage is fraught with disappointment, anger, bitterness, and a sense of failure. No one gets married with the idea that, hey, maybe it'll last, maybe it won't. Even the hardest-nosed cynic becomes a Pollyanna on his or her wedding day: we're full of hope and determination. We're relieved because we think we won't be afraid or lonely anymore. We see marriage as a magic fix for something that felt broken or incomplete in our lives. And, most of all, we're wearing highly tinted rose-colored glasses.

The little quirks in our beloved that seem so adorable now will metamorphose into fingernails on a chalkboard if those rose-colored glasses are ever lost or broken. And if we find this lifelong ally, this missing piece of our psychic puzzle, this holder-up of our heart suddenly sitting as far away from us as possible in a mediator's office, we're bound to have some strong feelings about it.

Since about half of all marriages end in divorce—not only in our culture but also in many other cultures around the world—it would seem highly sensible to reconceptualize divorce in such a way that friendships between ex-spouses become the rule rather than the exception. The people you'll read about in the following pages are pioneers of this new paradigm—the trailblazers and pattern breakers. This book is both a tribute to their courage and compassion, and a record of their journey, which may serve as a roadmap for others.

These are not stories of bitterness or failure, but messages of hope. We need to stop looking at divorce in such a narrow, negative way. The people in this book provide indisputable evidence that ex-spouses can break all the stereotypes and remain friends. But their stories also show that it is never simply easy to stay friends after being married and going through a divorce.

Some of the amicable exes you'll read about here had to put up with a great deal of disappointment, emotional pain, and even ill treatment. And yet none of them regret the expenditure of effort or the years of hard work and compromise, because they've given to themselves and their families a treasure beyond price. They are all—in their own ways, on their own terms—living happily ever after in a nurturing matrix of family ties.

The individuals interviewed for this book are people who have managed to exercise their right and duty to be happy while staying on the best of terms with their ex-spouse. They are no longer a couple. They are no longer lovers. But they are still friends. Each has worked to love and honor the other as a friend, just as they once vowed to love and honor each other as husband and wife. In some cases, their friendship is even richer than it was when they were married, because many of the tensions that caused them to opt for divorce are gone now.

These men and women all traveled along the same bumpy road to get to their present state of amicability, although they traveled it at various speeds and in different ways. But all were determined to stay on good terms (or to find good terms) following the uncomfortable transition that led up to and followed their divorce.

For many of them, this determination was fired by their mutual commitment to the welfare of their children. But even where children were not part of the picture, all of these ex-couples recognized qualities in their relationship that were too precious to lose completely. They found that many of these qualities—acceptance, familiarity, nurturing and being nurtured, knowing each other's histories in minute detail and liking each other anyway—could thrive outside the context of marriage. Some of them thrive much better there.

Many of these people told me that they and their ex-spouse are like siblings now: intimately connected, bound together for life, despite their many clashes. They are now and forever part of the same clan, mutually protective of their offspring, extended families, and each other.

These pioneers have rewritten the divorce script as we've known it—the script that says, "You lose, you're isolated, you've been cut loose from your anchor, cut off from the future you once imagined." They've found a way to stay connected to each other without staying married to each other. And in so doing, they've actually expanded, rather than diminished, their loving community and sense of belonging. Read on and feel inspired!

CHAPTER ONE

A Consideration of Marriage

THE COMPLEXITIES OF MARRIAGE and divorce were by no means invented in the twentieth century. As usual, a glance backward into history provides a useful and tonic perspective for students of contemporary life and mores.

A Brief History of Marriage

"The marriage vows have remained unchanged from the time when Henry VIII was busily beheading wives."

Only in the past hundred years or so have marriage and romance had anything to do with each other. In the time of the troubadours and courtly love, one's inamorata was never one's wife. Marriage was, and has mostly been throughout history, a political institution, used to link fortunes and bloodlines. It was a contractual agreement between families; the moral or emotional considerations of the two individuals involved were really beside the point.

The institution of marriage evolved to meet the needs of the wealthy—those with land, fortunes, or titles to pass on to their offspring. The central importance of fidelity in marriage had to do with inheritance rather than romantic preference. Thus it was only important for the female partner to be faithful: after all, no man wants to leave his fortunes and land to some other man's bastard. Chastity belts had more to do with banking than boinking. Really, it's no mistake that the two venues share so many of the same metaphors and vocabulary: we have trust funds and bonds of trust, investment bonds and marriage bonds, and brokers both for stocks and marriage. Mutual funds, Fidelity Investments, even premature withdrawals are phrases that lend themselves equally well to money or the marriage bed.

Sex has often been seen as part of the business— sometimes one of the burdens—of marriage. Among the titled gentry in eighteenth-century France, the marriage contract was likely to contain a provision designating the bride's *sigisbé,* or official lover. As long as the wife limited her romantic escapades to this person, no one minded. But straying with anyone else was grounds for divorce. (Her husband, not surprisingly, could have as many lovers as he pleased.)

At the other end of the social scale, people without rights or property most likely based their pairing-up decisions more on personal affinity than material considerations (except in cultures where marriages were always arranged). Marriage bonds between landless people were considered so irrelevant by those in power as to be disregarded entirely. Married couples sold into slavery were separated at the whim of their owners. The medieval *droit de seigneur* allowed the lord of the manor to deflower the new bride of any one of his serfs on their wedding night. (Presumably he picked up the tab for the party.)

The marriage vows—which made their first printed appearance in the *Sarum Manual of 1543* and were incorporated sixteen years later into the *Book of Common Prayer*—have remained unchanged from the time when Henry VIII was busily beheading wives. Women couldn't own or inherit property then; individual property ownership by married women wasn't legalized in Britain until 1869.[1]

In the context of those times, the marriage vows constituted a sensible bargain between husband and wife. The husband, who *could* own and inherit property, and thus had a means to make a living, agreed to take care of his wife and their offspring. In exchange, the wife assured the man through her promise of fidelity that his offspring were genetically related to him.

Our life span has almost tripled from the time when the marriage vows first came into vogue. As late as the 1700s in England, the average life expectancy for men was only thirty! The very idea of a marriage that would last for half a century or longer was completely outside the realm of possibility.

We not only live for a very long time, but also are encouraged to evolve as individuals—to grow and change and expand our horizons. Whereas the average Joe and Jane in Elizabethan times probably had little occasion and less desire to travel more than fifty miles from the place of their birth, we have the opportunity to live and travel all over the world. A man's firstborn children may be parents themselves before he starts another family with a new, much younger wife. If things keep going apace in reproductive technology, a woman who chooses to do so will also be able to start a new family in her golden years. We are on a continual course of self-improvement to look beautiful, be healthy and well informed, to enrich ourselves with experience and to live as long as possible. Our lives now are the moral and chronological equivalent of several seventeenth-century lives.

Our notions about what marriage is or should be are just as much an historical blip as go-go boots or bustles. Since around the start of the twentieth century, personal affinity has become the entire point of the marriage bond in many industrialized cultures. I've heard that in Japan, two corporate CEOs may still try to clinch the merger of their companies by arranging a marriage between their children. But the practice is frowned upon and frequently rebelled against by modern-minded offspring.

At this particular point in our time and history, pair-bonding is ruled by sentimental, cultural, and religious notions that often seem quite arbitrary and outdated. The institution of marriage, as we know it, seems to willfully ignore the real-life challenges and demands of "living happily ever after" as a long-term couple in a modern, complex world.

So much has changed in the four and a half centuries since the marriage vows were formulated, except the vows themselves. What does this mean for men and women linked by marriage today?

The Problem of Unchanging Vows

"We had a level of discourse that was not available to anybody else. And that's continued in the sense of still being family." — Jeremy

What would a marriage ceremony be without the echoed intonation of those time-honored phrases, "for richer for poorer, in sickness and in health" and, the clincher, "till death us do part"? These words are an established element of the marriage ritual, even in its most secular forms. But do we really consider the meaning of these words, or whether we can realistically expect to uphold the promises they delineate?

The marriage vows contain a presumption that both love and honor are unconditional—in other words, no matter how the conditions or circumstances surrounding the individuals in a marriage evolve, their love and honor for each other will endure. This is a very romantic and appealing notion that completely falls apart in the light of common sense.

As recently as two generations ago, a woman was expected to stay in a marriage even if her husband beat her. Mercifully, spousal violence is now recognized as an intolerable condition, at least in most Western industrialized nations. Women who stay in an abusive marriage are labeled as martyrs or masochists. Society encourages them to get out.

Using this one example alone, it's clear that love and honor are by their nature conditional. And yet there's no acknowledgment of this in the vows as most people take them. We don't say, "For richer for poorer—unless my spouse decides to quit his job as an investment banker and become a *sadhu* monk in India, living from whatever he can get in his begging bowl." No one gazes with dewy eyes at his beloved and says, "In sickness and in health— with the exception of psychotic breaks, episodes of pyromania, or a compulsion to have sex with everyone on my bowling team." No couple on their wedding day—at least none that I've heard of—winks at the person performing the ceremony and says, "Till death us do part—unless we become so tired of each other, or our habits become so grating, or we grow in such different directions, or one of us grows and the other one doesn't, so that staying together makes us feel more dead than alive and we wake up with dread each morning at having to face another day as a zombie in this pitiful charade."

Miriam and Jeremy, now in their fifties and the best of friends, had a marriage whose roots reached way back into childhood. Jeremy is an award-winning architect who makes his home in San Francisco. Miriam, a nurse, lives with her second husband, Lee, in nearby Napa County. The viability of their marriage ended four years after the birth of their son, when Jeremy admitted to himself and Miriam that he was gay. Both had to delve deeply into themselves to find acceptance and forgiveness. But the strength of their long-time friendship carried them through, and they are still the best of friends. Miriam told me, "No one else knows me like Jeremy does—and that's precious!" Jeremy added, "We had a level of discourse that was not available to anybody else. And that's continued in the sense of still being family."

The decision to give up on a marriage—or to pursue happiness and fulfillment outside a marriage—is born of desperation. We wanted it to work, but it hasn't. We wanted to be happy, but we weren't. We may try couples therapy, antidepressants, or individual counseling. We may spend years and years being unhappy and hoping that things will somehow change. But if we suddenly see our marriage for what it is, rather than what we wanted it to be—and if this isn't a vision we can live with forever and ever—we may very well look for a way out.

The Unspoken Marital Bargain

"I wanted to see what else the world had in store for me." — *Julie*

As Miriam and Jeremy discovered, life changes can well lead to the end of a marriage.

Julie and Michael, both professional ballet

dancers, had been immersed in the dance world together since the time they met, when Julie was fourteen and Michael was twenty. They eventually married, living together as husband and wife, and working as dance partners on the stage. After nine years of marriage, as Julie approached her thirtieth birthday, she made the difficult choice to end her professional career as a ballerina. She remembers, "I was trying to decide whether or not I wanted to continue dancing."

Being dancers together was part of the unspoken marital bargain she and Michael had made. "I wanted to see what else the world had in store for me," Julie told me. "I think I was starting to grow up in a different way. I just remember feeling like I wasn't doing the inner work that I needed and wanted to do as a human being. I was so consumed by all this ballet stuff that I wasn't paying attention to some other areas of growth."

Julie had been dancing with serious focus since the age of six; ballet was and still is Michael's passion. "Our marriage really fell apart after I stopped dancing," Julie continued. "It felt like we didn't have as much to share if I wasn't dancing, that he wanted a partner who could share that life with him."

Julie and Michael have managed to forge a close and vivid relationship as friends—along with Michael's second wife, Lara, who is also a dancer. Experience taught them that the success of love within a marriage, like life itself, is always conditional. Marriages live and die not only by the promises we make at our wedding ceremonies, but by the unspoken marital bargains between us.

I'm Not You and You're Not Me—What an Awful Surprise!

"He kept describing this mythical woman to me, and I finally realized that what he wanted was simply a female version of himself."
— Samantha

The fatal affront to the marital bond is often the realization that you will never be able to fulfill each other's needs. Who you thought your spouse was at the beginning may turn out to be nothing more than a fond romantic projection.

When you meet people for the first time, you can usually hear and see them with a fair degree of clarity. But once you fall in love—and especially after you've become lovers—that clarity begins to fade. Matt McKay, a psychologist and author, says that it's as if suddenly there's Vaseline smeared on your camera lens. You start to see the other person in soft focus. Things that are less pleasing to you get pushed into your peripheral vision, where you barely see them at all. You convince yourself that certain things you see and hear aren't really there or are only ephemeral.

Realizing that you're actually separate and distinct people can be one of the greatest challenges in a marriage. If you know what you like, it's far too easy to assume that your spouse loves all the same things you do. That's the great, destructive illusion. That's Homer Simpson giving Marge a bowling ball for her birthday.

Marital disillusionment often entails really seeing and acknowledging your differences and separateness for the first time. That's what happened to Samantha and Jake, who were married for six years and got divorced when their daughter was in kindergarten.

Samantha ended up going back to school and becoming a physician. She and Jake are still bound together in a close co-parenting relationship, even though they no longer live together as husband and wife. Samantha shared some of her insights on the difference question: "In the final two years of our marriage, Jake would give me presents that showed how completely clueless he was about where he ended and I began. One birthday, it was a fishing rod and tackle. For Valentine's Day that last year, he gave me a Swiss Army knife." She paused, then added, "He'd give me these presents, and then he'd complain bitterly that I wasn't the sort of woman who would really like them. He kept describing this mythical woman to me, and I finally realized that what he wanted was simply a female version of himself."

Sometimes the marriage of opposites can work—just ask Jack Sprat and his wife. But often the differences that lend spice to a romance are the very factors that can cause a marriage to fail.

Unfortunately, no one has figured out yet which differences are okay and which are deadly in a marriage. I suspect, though, that it's not the differences themselves that make or break a marriage— after all, the only way to find a romantic partner who likes all the same things you do is to look into a mirror and give yourself a big kiss!

Ellen, a social worker and child advocate, did her best to gloss over the differences between her and her husband Ernie. Wildly energetic, Ellen balances a more-than-full-time job with full-time motherhood, copious volunteer work, membership on a softball team, and a passion for tap dancing. Ernie, whom she loved dearly, preferred being a couch potato in his spare time. "Ernie's friends were totally blown away that I got him to go backpacking," she told me. "I never admitted that I did so by carrying a six-pack of beer and some pot for him, and that I carefully researched camping destinations for distance, difficulty of access, and a fabulous vista, which would be the carrot at the end of the stick."

The differences between Ellen and Ernie ran deeper than their outlook on athletic pursuits. Ellen is very clear and articulate about why their marriage ended. She said simply, "Ernie just didn't feel like being married anymore. He loved me deeply but could not function within the confines of a marital bond, which he found constricting and uncomfortable."

Differences, as Ellen learned, often lead to conflict. But conflict itself doesn't necessarily destroy a marriage. The latest research, from longitudinal studies by John Gottman, indicates that it's not so much how you handle conflict that predicts whether your marriage will last, but whether you and your spouse handle conflict in the same way.[2] For instance, two people who tend to sweep things under the rug have a better prognosis than a couple in which one person is a rug sweeper and the other favors direct confrontation.

We're bound to be different from our spouse— "Vive la différence!" the French are fond of saying. Rather, it's the way in which we reconcile our differences and resolve our conflicts that heads us on the path either to his-and-hers cemetery plots or divorce court.

The Inherent Difficulties of Marriages

"You look a lot like someone I used to be married to!" — *Edie*

For Miriam and Jeremy, and Julie and Michael, friendship rather than marriage turned out to be a better long-term modality for their relationship.

Marriage is certainly the messiest and most intimate mutual connection that two human beings can have. Maybe in Victorian times, when some people lived in great big houses and husbands and wives had separate bedrooms, it was possible to keep some secrets from each other—and to maintain some romantic allure. In those days, a middle- or upper-class woman would emerge from her boudoir fully dressed in all her finery for a social outing with her husband. Nowadays, with shared bedrooms and bathrooms, every secret of a woman's toilette is revealed. A brand-new husband may watch in either fascination or horror as his lovely bride shaves her underarms and flosses her teeth.

I remember a college friend confiding his horror at waking up with the cocktail waitress of his dreams only to see the makeup-blackened crusts of sleep in the corners of her eyes. What agony to discover that the love of your life snores like a pig that's swallowed a teakettle, opens cabinets but seems congenitally incapable of closing them, or—in true hunter fashion—can't see anything in your house except what's moving, suffering from what a very clever comedienne has dubbed "male pattern blindness."[3]

Men who, pulling on their trousers and running their hands through their hair, can get ready to go out to breakfast in fifteen seconds flat, must wait sixty times that long while their mates do whatever it is that women must do before they feel prepared to meet the public. And many a woman looks on in stupefied amazement and envy as her partner in life sits contently reading magazines smack at the center of domestic disaster—dirty dishes, clothing, diapers, newspapers, dust bunnies, and junk mail. It's completely amazing to me that romantic attachment can withstand the relentless onslaught of intimacy that cohabitation entails.

Yet there is also something tremendously attractive in the notion of being so witnessed and still loved by another human being. Who else in the world knows exactly the order in which you make your preparations to go to bed, which side you prefer to sleep on, whether or not you get up in the middle of the night to pee, and that *vichyssoise* always gives you gas? Who else, but someone to whom you've been married, knows what you like to drink or eat or do first thing in the morning, which section of the paper you start with, and whether or not you ever blow your nose while you're washing your face? Who, except someone who truly cares, will know that anything you say between four and five in the morning—no matter how hostile or accusing or desperate—is best answered with a snuggle and a soothing murmur of, "It'll all look much different to you in a couple of hours."

The odd thing about breaking up is that the intimate knowledge remains—you still know each other as only another spouse can know you. Upon seeing my father for the first time in a decade at a family reunion, my mother walked gamely up to him and said, "You look a lot like someone I used to be married to!" And in her laugh and his acknowledging smile, their twenty-four-year-long intimate history seemed to hang in the air for a moment, waving like a banner. Both of them feel that the happiest parts of their lives started after their divorce. But the knowledge of each other they share—to say nothing of the three children and four grandchildren—is a thread that keeps them, however tenuously, connected. Although they live many hundreds of miles away from each other, I find that they're still oddly in synchrony, often laughing at the same jokes, loving the same movies, stirred by their many shared memories. And each of them is deeply grateful not to be married to the other any longer.

The Male-Female Thing

"A man marries a woman hoping she'll never change, but she always does. A woman marries a man hoping he'll change, but he never does." —Anonymous

A great deal of research (and much speculation) has been lavished on the psychological differences between men and women, and the ways in which these differences are communicated. Given my gender, my understanding of the male point of view is imperfect. But from what I've gathered from my spies, I've drawn the conclusion that men are much more visually oriented than women when it comes to love. Women long for romance —for connection, for the sense of being witnessed and understood, for appreciation. Men lust after beautiful, alluring images with which they can merge—either in reality or, barring that, in their imagination.

Men fall in love with an image. Women fall in love with something invisible that lurks inside a man. A man sees a woman for who he thinks she is. A woman sees a man for who she thinks he can become. Men fall in love with surfaces. Women fall in love with potential.

Eventual disappointment is built into both approaches. The man may be mistaken in his idea or projection about who this woman really is. Or he may be more or less right—in the moment. But who a woman is—what she likes doing, what is most important to her, what her goals are—is a fluid process rather than something written forever in stone. A young woman of twenty has radically different needs and goals than the same woman ten or twenty years later. Hence, a man marries a woman hoping she'll never change, but she always does.

On the other hand, it's often true that a woman marries a man hoping he'll change, but he almost never does—at least not within the desired time-frame. The young woman who marries a young man with the idea of just giving him a tweak here and there to bring about desirable changes is bound to be disappointed—that is, unless she's ready to wait about twenty years.

Obviously, the fixer-upper approach to shopping for a mate has inherent and overwhelming pitfalls. If a woman can't imagine really living in this house with all its oddities and inconveniences and imperfections—the marvelous vistas blocked by completely unnecessary walls, the leaky roof, the foundation that so obviously needs shoring up, and the kitchen that is simply crying out for a remodel—she'd better think long and hard before she coughs up the money for the down payment.

It's my own private theory that most males in Western industrialized society don't leave boyhood until they're well into their forties. This painful passage to manhood—many males of the species are only carried through that door kicking and screaming—is what we commonly refer to as "the male midlife crisis."

Women tend to feel ready for marriage about twenty years before their male counterparts. Marrying a much older man might seem like a logical solution up front, but holds its own compelling challenges down the line.

The achievement of living happily ever after as husband and wife needs to be more fully appreciated and understood. Getting married is easy. Staying married—and feeling whole and fulfilled within that relationship—is not only difficult, but it's sometimes simply out of our control, however honorable our intentions.

Living Happily Ever After Anyway

"I adore him, I love him—but he's a very difficult, selfish, self-centered man." — Muriel

Muriel and her ex-husband Max, both in their seventies, are internationally known in the world of fine arts—she's a painter, he's a conductor. Muriel was absolutely dedicated to the notion of keeping Max actively involved in their son Federico's life, no matter how badly she was feeling at any given time about Max walking out on their marriage. She also clearly harbors very special feelings for him. "I adore him, I love him," she said, speaking of the man from whom she's been divorced now for over thirty years, "but he's a very difficult, selfish, self-centered man."

Muriel has the equivalent of another full-time career as a volunteer coordinator for foster children and hospice programs in and around Boston. Her patience and forbearance with Max through the years have richly paid off. They now have a friendship that they both deeply cherish. Their new, reconfigured, extended family—including

Max's young wife, Jeannette, their seven-year-old son, and Federico's wife and three-year-old daughter—spend Thanksgiving and Christmas together whenever schedules and geography allow.

Muriel was willing to give two hundred percent to keep her family closely bound even after her marriage fell apart. Despite the many humiliations she suffered because of Max's insensitivity to pretty much anyone's feelings but his own, she persisted in her belief that her life—and her son's—would be enhanced by Max's continuing presence.

Muriel had to weigh many factors in committing herself to an ongoing, amicable relationship with her ex-husband. She knew as well as anyone else that there are some marital choices so bad—and some people so hopelessly destructive, angry, cruel, or simply damaged—that no one with an ounce of self-esteem would want an ongoing relationship with them. Such exes are best consigned to the compost pile before you move on.

But I think it's incumbent on every divorced person—especially those with children—to look with a magnifying glass, if necessary, for the slightest trace of goodness and worth in his or her former spouse—and then to build whatever relationship is possible on these qualities, even if they're in short supply.

The road to an amicable relationship is usually a rocky one. As you'll see in the next chapter, even the chummiest exes needed to travel over that road before reaching a place where they could build a friendship upon the ruins of their marriage.

CHAPTER TWO

Navigating the Rocky Road from Divorce to Friendship

"There were no models, recipes, or guidebooks for us to follow. We were pioneering an unknown territory." — Joan

NO MATTER HOW civilized the parties involved, the transition between being married and being ex-spouses necessitates travel over a rocky road. Even the most adorably linked exes in this book had to negotiate that neglected section of life's highway, where the potholes are as deep as graves and spew the sulphurous odors of hell itself. Franny, who has been devoted to her ex-husband, Paul, for the past twenty years, says that in the first five months after their divorce, "we knew we were supposed to not like each other at that point—so we didn't!"

This messy transition period can last for shorter or longer stretches of time—from a few months to forever for the ex-spouses who never get over what happened to their dreams.

The road to amicability following a divorce is littered with the painful emotions of both spouses as they grapple with the changing reality of their status in the world. We learn to define ourselves in relationship to our marital partner, whether as ally or victim. Without that partner, we may have very little idea for quite a while about who in blazes we are by ourselves.

Daphne Rose Kingma writes in *Coming Apart*, "It is our relationships, more than anything else in our lives, which help us accomplish the developmental tasks through which we define ourselves. That's why we choose the people we do and that's why they choose us. That's why relationships begin and end."[1] What a shock it is—and what an opportunity—to need to suddenly redefine yourself independently of the light and shadow formerly cast by your spouse!

"I have watched," writes Kingma, "as time and again, after anguishing crises in self-esteem, my clients emerged from their shattered relationships with enhanced self-images, redefined careers, recaptured creativity, pared-down, toned-up bodies, bad habits lost, new habits gained—in short, transformed identities."[2]

As you limp or race down that road into the rest of your life, you may experience anger and/or guilt, depending on what your role was in initiating the separation. Following this, there seems to be an inevitable stretch of the road—even a year or two into the separation—reserved for grieving. *What happened to the marriage I once believed in with all my heart? What happened to the happy family I always planned to be part of?*

The terrain eventually changes, and you find yourself in the territory of healing. You lick your wounds. Like a sick cat, you find a warm place in the tall grass by the side of the road to hunker down and let the sunlight wash over you. The next nearest town, a short ride from healing, is forgiveness. You stop here and dump out your ashtrays and garbage sacks. You find a laundromat and wash all your clothes, even if it means standing around naked in the fresh, sweet air while they dry.

When you've dumped all your trash and washed the dirt of the road out of your clothes, you take a plunge in a beautiful little river called insight. The water is clear and bracingly cold. Lots of old ideas get washed away here. Your eyes get a good wash, too, and when you look down into one of insight's clear pools, where the water is still and deep, you see a whole new reflection staring back at you. The face you see isn't angry or bitter. It's a face that has suffered, that has felt deeply; but it's somehow serene.

If your ex-spouse were to kneel beside you, looking down into the clear, reflective waters, he or she would also look amazingly different to you. You would see yourselves as two distinct yet worthy human beings. Things that bothered you before about your spouse are still visible; but rather than passing judgment or feeling uncomfortable, you simply take these things in as information. You can see the inner and outer beauty of your ex-spouse without needing to possess it in any way. You do not want to change this person any more than you would want to change a tree or a rock or a butterfly.

Because you have been so intimately connected and have gone through so much together, you can see this person very clearly, with a connoisseur's appreciation. If this is the mother or father of your children, you are very, very glad.

You both rise up from gazing down into the pool, look at each other, and smile. You recognize an opportunity. This person is uniquely suited to be one of your dearest friends. You may not see each other as often as you see your other friends, but there will always be a sweet, invisible thread tying you together.

You wave or shake hands or give each other a hug. And then you each get on with the rest of your life. You know you'll never be as alone in the world as someone who's never been married.

First Stop: Anger

"The key, for me, came in acceptance—easy to say but oh so hard to really do! For those unhappy years, I constantly thought, 'How can he do that? How can he act that way?' My judgments of him created so much bad feeling."
— *Helena*

After ten years of marriage, four years after the birth of their daughter, Jenny, Jonathan announced to Sybil that he'd fallen in love with someone named Bob. Talk about your dreams falling apart! "I was

....
33

really angry when he was going through all of this," said Sybil, who works as an account executive for a newspaper in Santa Fe, New Mexico, "because I didn't have a husband, basically, or a lover, or anything."

Learning that your spouse is gay creates a lot of emotions, but anger is bound to be part of the brew. Sybil's words were echoed by Miriam, whose revelation about her husband, Jeremy, came nearly a generation earlier. "When the knowledge first hit me of what was really happening, then it was like, 'Oh, s____!' It took a while to defuse that, because I was angry and I didn't want to talk to Jeremy for a while. It didn't last...I know that one time I sort of lashed out, and I said that I didn't want our son, Jason, to be around him. That was my angry outburst."

Adair, a talented San Francisco newspaper writer, told me about the aftermath of her divorce. "It wasn't all that amicable at first. The first time I came over with a boyfriend, my ex-husband wasn't exactly a happy camper." Anger, at this stage, can run the gamut from direct expression to careful suppression.

Joel, a biologist from Idaho, told me about his

experience. "Our breakup was not accompanied by a lot of fighting, as Judy and I are both non-confrontational by nature. I think what made our divorce easier than most that I've heard about is that we never got to the point of hating each other. When it was clear that things would not improve between us, I wanted to move on and I suspect Judy did, too. That isn't to say that I didn't feel some bitterness, but that actually came later on for me, and I segregated those feelings as best as I could from our subsequent relationship."

Colin, a television producer, and his ex-spouse drove through postmarital anger without ever stopping. He wrote to me from Los Angeles: "Our motivation was simple: we would honor our lives together and never harm each other if we could possibly avoid it. The alternative: destructive and self-destructive rage, which we considered unacceptable. Beyond the agony of parting—a bit like vivisection—there was little residual animosity, because we wanted to avoid it."

Dealing with anger for many is not as easy as it was for Colin and his ex-wife. Helena, an epidemiologist who works in Washington, DC, wrote, "When Peter and I lived together, there was much discord, tension, bickering. I regret that very much, especially its impact on our young teenage son. Several years of bitterness, anger, and discord followed the divorce. The key, for me, came in acceptance—easy to say, but oh so hard to really do! For those unhappy years, I constantly thought, 'How can he do that? How can he act that way?' My judgments of him created so much bad feeling."

Joan and Ritch adore each other now. But the transition from husband and wife to exes was difficult, even for them. "I was so angry," Joan told me. "Ritch's denial wouldn't let him see what I was angry about. And that made me all the angrier! I had no ability to manage my anger, and he had no ability to see through his denial. I was loaded with resentment and hostility when I left."

A San Francisco restaurateur, Olivia, describes the first leg of her post-separation journey: "It wasn't that really awful, bitter, attacking or blaming kind of stuff, but it was very uncomfortable. One person wants to stay married, and the other person doesn't. It took Mike a while to stop being angry at me."

Ellen's perspective is somewhat different from everyone else's here, because Ernie, who gave her so much cause to be angry, is no longer alive. "It's interesting, psychologically speaking," Ellen wrote to me, "that it's so much harder to remember all the negative and frustrating aspects of this man than to remember all the positives. I felt the pain of his needing to live separately so keenly for the first few years, even with our co-parenting of Charlotte. It took a lot of support from friends and family to realize that it was okay for me to be angry about these things, and that taking care of myself (via a good lawyer, a therapist and some financial counseling) didn't make me a jerk or a bad co-parent/mother. *Au contraire*, I did what I needed to in order to worry less, protect my child and myself from further trauma, and get over the pain and down to the task of re-negotiating all of our respective lives."

Julie talked about the beginning of her transition from being Michael's wife and dancing partner to being a retired ballerina. Within four months of their divorce, Michael had become romantically involved with Lara, another dancer; and the new relationship Julie was in was not working out. "That was the hard year," Julie told me, "because my life wasn't going so well. Sometimes I'd go back to Michael for some kind of comfort—not wanting necessarily to get back together, but just wanting some help. Sometimes," Julie continued, "we'd have some harsh words. I was asking him for things that he couldn't or shouldn't have to give. And I think I might have even been questioning some things—and it was too late. It was a really scary time for me."

The involvement of an ex-spouse with another person is challenging for most people, but it is even more challenging when friends are involved. Bianca and Dorian, Molly and Noah described the remarkable journey that brought them together again as two newly reconfigured couples with all their friendships intact. Bianca and Molly work together as practitioners of a specialized form of healing bodywork. That's how they met and became best friends. Their work also provided the occasion for Bianca, who lived in Sonoma County, to frequently spend weekends at Molly's house in Berkeley, where she grew close both to Molly's husband, Dorian, and their two children. Unwittingly, Bianca and Dorian fell in love. Soon afterwards, Molly and Noah acknowledged a slow-brewing but deep affinity.

"Dorian and I were reacting a lot to each other through hurt feelings," Molly told me. "But since we had kids, we knew right away, for their sake, we needed to maintain some unity. It forced us to dig down inside and go beyond whatever personality stuff was on the surface."

Dorian and Molly's children, Caitlin and Flynn, are attractive, bright, and obviously well-adjusted —the type of children that other kids' parents love to welcome into their home. At nine and twelve, they seem to have a remarkable, almost instinctual understanding of the forces of love that broke their family into its component parts, then rearranged them into a new but equally loving configuration. Any parents would feel happy and proud to have two such children. But each member of the group had to work through feelings of anger before arriving at reconciliation. "It was difficult for everyone in the beginning," said Dorian.

Even if you manage to speed through anger, like Colin and his ex did, without stopping, you'll still notice the road sign, and you'll still give it a nod. It's an unavoidable place along the path to amicability. Because we're human beings and not angels or birds with wings, or moles that can tunnel underground without coming up for air, every one of us has to pass through anger in one way or another. It's a natural and inevitable part of breaking up. And you have to get rid of your anger—by taking a good look at it and then throwing it away, or even by choosing to ignore it, burying it in the deepest reaches of your personal compost pile— before you and your ex can be friends again.

Next Stop: Grieving

*"**I** cried a lot. I talked to friends. My heart was broken. And I know hers was, too."*
— Ritch

Sybil and Jonathan are the best of friends now, successfully co-parenting their daughter, Jenny. But their transition—from husband and wife to cooperative co-parents and friends after Jonathan came out of the closet—required them both to reach deeply into themselves for reserves of courage and compassion. "I grieved and still do," Sybil told me. "I grieved over the loss of my marriage."

David, who consults for high-tech firms in the Silicon Valley, described his feelings after he and

Susan stopped living together and the "transition relationship"—the young woman he'd gotten involved with before the break-up with Susan—also fell apart. "I was very unhappy. I'd lost both of these women, and my life was ruined!"

Muriel, the internationally exhibited painter, now in her early 70s, turned her anger inward as depression over the years. She had a lot of grieving to work through before she and Max reached their present, apparently serene state of amicability.

Muriel recounted one of the lower points in their journey: "Max came home and said that he needed to go away and think about if he wanted to leave or not. He said, 'I'll write you and let you know what my decision is.' Muriel laughed enormously here, which throughout our interview signaled particularly anguished feelings. "My son and I would come home for lunch every day from school—I was working as a teacher's aide at his school then—to see if there was any mail from Max. We came home and there was this long letter from him saying that he definitely wanted to get a divorce."

Muriel went through several major depressions. "I think the big one," she told me, "was when

Federico went away to college. And I thought, 'My life is over. The only thing I've been successful as is a mother. And now I'm not needed anymore.' And I went into a really bad depression then."

It's so hard to comprehend the darkness and pain Muriel went through to get to the marvelous relationship she now has with Max. In part because she was determined to keep Max in their son's life— but also because she really loves Max—Muriel never gave up, never gave in to bitterness or disappointment or wounded pride. She kept plugging away at creating a relationship between all three of them that would work. When Max, fairly late in life, remarried and had another child, Muriel included them in her loving constellation. Where Max was stubborn and inflexible, Muriel was open-minded and fluid. She was yin to his yang, which was what ultimately allowed them to stay in the circle together.

Thirty-nine-year-old Julie told me about her passage through grieving after she left the ballet stage and she and her dancer husband Michael got a divorce. "Within a year, everything fell apart. I suffered a major identity crash. I went through this seven-year odyssey of trying to find out who I was in this world, and it has not been easy. I felt like I wanted to strip away everything that defined me and see who I was without all of the labels—a dancer, a wife—but I didn't realize it was going to be as hard as it was."

I felt nothing but admiration for Julie as she spoke about this painful time. Did she know, I wondered, that she and Michael and his new wife, Lara, would eventually become the best of friends? "The first year after our divorce," she told me, "Michael and I were not very close. It was a painful year. I didn't have any idea what it was going to be like for us to be divorced. I imagined that we were going to be able to stay really close and everything. But we had a year where we weren't that close."

When I interviewed Julie, Michael, and Lara together, I was struck by the love and respect they clearly have for each other, and by the honesty and openness of their relationships—husband to wife, spouse to ex-spouse, first wife to second wife. Like Muriel, Julie was bound and determined to remain friends with her ex. And Lara, who is kind and sensitive and generous despite her characterization of herself as "a tough cookie," made this as easy for

Julie as it could possibly be, under the circumstances. But the circumstances themselves were far from easy. Julie needed time—and wisely took the time she needed—to grieve.

Despite the seemingly miraculous ease and symmetry of their marital "switch," Dorian and Bianca, and Molly and Noah also had to put in their time along the grieving road. Molly said, "A close friend—one who later presided over our marriage ceremony—cautioned me that moving so quickly from the end of one relationship into another would have its emotional repercussions. She suggested that some time alone to take stock might be appropriate. Years into my new marriage I saw that this had been good advice, because feelings of loss and grief did surface and call for some acknowledgment." Molly continued, "For me the grief was about not being able to make my marriage with Dorian work. I love Dorian very much, and I thought that we'd always be married. It's like having a wound that doesn't heal. It's not a wound that I wouldn't want, or hasn't been worth it, but it doesn't go away either. Changing partners was not something any of us took lightly."

Ellen told me, "Once Ernie decided that he did,

in fact, want a formal 'marital liberation,' it became much harder for me to do activities conjointly, although we maintained a fifty-fifty shared custody arrangement that, compared to most of my divorcing friends' situations, was very fluid and flexible in terms of accommodating everyone's needs. Still, I cried nearly every time I dropped Charlotte off at his apartment and, despite all outward appearances, was truly grieving the loss of our former way of being close."

Samantha, who reports that she was the oldest person in her graduating class at UC San Francisco Medical School, is now an OB/GYN at a clinic in East Oakland. "I'm a person who tends to go through transitions rapidly and fairly easily," she told me. "I've found it hard in the past to realize that not everyone is wired this way. Jake, I know, has been having a much harder time than I have moving through the stages of our journey from spouses to friendly and cooperative co-parents. I keep trying to remember to tell myself to slow down, not to expect him to be able to race through it all side by side with me. A counselor told me this when we were first going through the separation, when Jake was so horribly depressed and agitated at the same time. She practically had to yell at me, 'Slow down! Give him time!'"

Grief is an especially bumpy, ill-lit and treacherous stretch of highway. Some people find ways to travel along it quickly, madly gripping the steering wheel as they barrel along, closing their eyes and praying for the next signpost to appear. Others travel the road with no vehicle at all to protect them or speed them on their way. Some people head down that highway on their hands and knees. There's maybe no controlling how long it takes or how you do it. You've just got to have faith that everyone, given enough time, can eventually get to the end of that part of the road.

Third Stop: Healing

*"**R**itch and I were saved, above all else, by our willingness to feel everything—to go through all of whatever it was that came up and still stay in relationship after our divorce." — Joan*

There is no one way to heal, no universal prescription that will relieve the pain and sense of failure that people inevitably feel in the aftermath of a divorce. Each of the people I interviewed had to find the medicine inside themselves. It's sort of like building up antibodies to a disease—only your body can make the ones that will work for you.

I asked Muriel how she had dealt with her depression when her son left for college. "I was in the hospital for two weeks," she told me. "I don't think I needed to be, though. I could have spent two weeks in my studio, and it would have done the same thing for me—and, yes, I have wonderful friends."

Work, as Muriel suggested, can play a role in healing. For some, a sense of a power beyond them helps. I was, for example, so struck by the description of healing contained in Bianca's initial letter to me: "Perhaps the strongest impression I have of those confusing, tumultuous months is that it all happened as if the fateful and benevolent hand of Existence reached out, rearranged us (having provided each of us with certain qualities and tools that were needed to move us, as a group, through all the changes), and gave us a fabulous opportunity not only to enter into new, more nurturing relationships, but also to do so under circumstances that supported us, over and over, to let go of our reactive thoughts and feelings in favor of our larger, common aim, which was to go through whatever we had to go through with as little hurt to the children as possible.

"As it turned out, I came back to live in the city, and Molly went to live in my peaceful country home. About three years ago, Molly married Noah and I married Dorian. The weddings were at a beautiful place in the countryside, outdoors, both on the same beautiful, sunny day and with one big wedding cake and all the same guests."

Ellen told me how her healing journey began after Ernie walked out on her in the midst of their daughter Charlotte's life-threatening medical problems. "I ultimately turned to a support group for parents of kids with cardiac conditions for the support I so desperately wanted and needed from him.

"Once I made those shifts in thinking and, eventually, in feelings, too, we were able to proceed toward a remake of our relationship, with expectations that were more realistic and less of a psychological 'set-up' for me. It was also after that that our co-parenting therapy became really quite productive, and our capacity to resolve issues greatly increased.

"I do not mean to make any of this sound simple or to trivialize the pain, anxiety about the future, or concern I had for Charlotte's well-being. Had Ernie not become ill shortly thereafter, who knows? I could still be harboring more of the negative feelings of being the victimized ex. But it is hard for me now to think of him as the callous, narcissistic hippie that he seemed to be at the time he announced his intention to leave the marriage. Instead, I think that if he were alive, our connectedness may have even allowed us to be together as a family, even if he needed to live elsewhere. Where this fantasy stops, and reality begins, is anyone's guess."

Joan wrote to me from her home in Kauai about her journey with Ritch along the healing road. Joan is, by profession, a healer—which perhaps makes her especially able to register her own experience there. "Above all else," Joan wrote, "we were helped by our willingness to feel everything —to go through all of whatever it was that came up and still stay in relationship. To honor the sacredness of this love that brought us together and bonded us through our hearts. And still be willing to feel the hate or the rage or the disgust or the distrust. Learning from our mistakes. And apologizing. Finding the time to be together. Refining our friendship. Always being there for each other whenever the other needed us." Joan continued, "I can remember many a very nasty fight on the phone when one of us would hang up, beside ourselves with anger. But before the night was over, one of us would call back just to check in, say the worst had passed, and bring whatever degree of softness and love that was now possible (no matter how big or small that might be) back into the arena."

The point, I think, is not how fast you can heal or how creative you can be resisting the temptation to succumb to anger, grief, or despair. It's not a question of how stubborn you can be, or how resilient or saintlike. The point made by these stories, I think, is simply this: no matter how horrendous the rift, how gaping the wound, no matter how much your heart is bleeding or your blood is boiling, healing is always possible. The path through the jungle of your own painful emotions may be extremely hard to find, but there is a path, however hidden. You can still get to the path of healing. No matter how much time has passed, it's not too late. As long as you and your ex are still breathing, you can still find a way to honor both the love that brought you together and the needs that caused you to part.

Fourth Stop: Forgiveness

"Why would I want to dismiss Molly from my life, the mother of my children, this woman whom I loved so much that we married?" — Dorian

Forgiveness can be very hard to find and, in fact, it will not take root and blossom until its time has come. It can't be forced or hurried, or otherwise pressured into existence. And forgiveness, I firmly believe, will only follow healing.

Forgiveness requires the absence of an agenda. To forgive a spouse who has abandoned you or let you down in some other way perhaps requires you to no longer need anything from him or her. Forgiveness requires you, on some level at least, to be self-sufficient and whole. It's very difficult to find forgiveness from a position of vulnerability and need.

Josie, an archaeologist, wrote to me from England: "I am very pleased that Noël is happy with his present life and second family—he seems to have a great talent in producing excellent daughters. I too have found much fulfillment in my current life."

For Miriam, whose husband Jeremy came out of the closet after a lifelong friendship and many years of marriage to her, forgiveness and acceptance were the only option. "Jeremy was part of my life for so long!" she told me, her voice filled with feeling. "I figured that if this is the way it's going to be, then this is the way it is. I wasn't about to lose this friendship that had been going on forever and that meant so much to me."

Dorian, Bianca, Molly and Noah couldn't possibly blame one another without each blaming themselves. Each wife chose the other's husband over her own. Each individual in the quartet was wounded, but each was also rewarded with a better match spiritually and a more emotionally rewarding marriage.

Dorian wrote to me, "One of the greatest benefits of the 'Big Divorce' was that it broke my heart. For me, to go through life with a broken heart is to be a little more open, a little more receptive, and a little less willing to believe in my 'version' or my 'interpretation' of events. Almost everyone I have ever admired has had some wisdom, some depth, some sorrow that has come from living life fully—a life that can fill you with happiness but break your heart too. Why would I want to dismiss Molly from my life, the mother of my children, this woman whom I loved so much that we married? My broken heart makes it possible for me to walk in her shoes, to hear her, to include her. And this openness allows love to exist between us in a different way, one where, although we are not still married, we are still connected forever.

"The biggest shock, though, was how surprised and dumbfounded almost everybody was that we—the four of us—could go through a separation and not become enemies. That process—friends to enemies—seems to be accepted as a natural part of the way things are and the way things have to be. The interesting thing is that we felt that we were doing it the natural and normal way—so normal, in fact, that there seemed to be support, seen and unseen, for us at every step of the way."

As a therapist, Joan was able to see in retrospect

that she and Ritch completed an important developmental task in their passionate love affair and intense but stormy marriage to each other. In this context, for Joan—and for Ritch as well—there was no blame. In fact, despite the heartbreak for both of them, they see their relationship in all its aspects as a cause for gratitude and celebration.

As Joan put it, "We ultimately realized that there was nothing really to forgive—we in fact had co-created all that caused us pain as well as all that brought us pleasure. No matter how much deprivation I experienced within the pattern of our dysfunction, the truth was Ritch gave me over and over the one thing he was meant to give me, the thing that I was needing the most. He gave me the gift of his unconditional love."

Rather than forgive and forget, I think it is one of our special privileges as human beings to forgive and remember. As Samantha wrote to me, "Even though it may sound strange, it makes me feel good to remember the love that brought me and Jake together—the gentleness I saw in him, the unconditional, embracing quality of his love. It doesn't really matter that a lot of the love I saw was somewhat of a projection, somewhat of a fantasy.

Jake was there for me, even if only as a sort of benign screen onto which I could project and explore my needs. He had his own stuff going on inside him, his own enormous sense of pain and deprivation—and I can only hope that I also healed him in some way.

"Certainly our child has been the best and most important thing that life has given either of us—and life has been very generous to us both. I know that we both take pride and satisfaction in knowing that it was us—and our love—that brought our daughter into the world. She's living proof that our time together wasn't in any way wasted time or a wrong turn or a mistake. I think, for both of us, when we look at our daughter, the whole issue of blame and forgiveness simply disappears."

Forgiveness isn't so much a gift to your ex as it is a gift to yourself—when you find forgiveness and embrace it, you will finally be ready to move on.

Fifth Stop: Insight

*"**I**f you love, respect, and value the person you married after you're no longer living as husband and wife, that's almost a purer, maybe*

*a higher form of love. You can look and see who
that person really is, and you have a choice
about how you feel. It's a conscious, open-eyed
kind of love rather than the kind of love where
you close your eyes and hope for the best."*
— *Samantha*

Courtship is a time of learning of each other's
charms. Marriage is a process of uncovering each
other's secrets, both good and bad. And in divorce,
ironically enough, we open a window on our
innermost nature, both for ourselves and our ex-
spouse to see. It was some misogynistic pundit or
other who said, "You really never know a woman
until you meet her in divorce court." But the tru-
ism applies equally to both genders.

Perhaps it's impossible to see all sides of another
person when you're joined at the hip in marriage.
Perhaps it takes the perspective afforded by separation to see clearly both your partner and the marriage you made together.

This *satori*—this moment of insight—seems to
be the final stop along the rocky road from the end
of a marriage to the beginning of an amicable relationship as ex-spouses. Maybe without this essen-

tial understanding about what happened and why, the marriage bond is never cleanly broken. People who have not divorced amicably carry their ex-spouse with them into their future as a poisonous, polluting—albeit ghostlike—presence. This ghost-spouse may inject fear and mistrust into new relationships. It can make you close off certain parts of your past for fear of looking at the skeletons in the closet there, of remembering the ugliness. It can be like a bitter vegetable added to life's stew, tainting the flavor of the whole thing.

After anger, after grieving, after healing, after forgiveness, insight was the final destination for all of the amicable exes I interviewed—and from there, the road branched out for them in many different but equally exciting directions.

Speaking of the aftermath of his marriage, Jeremy said, "I think one of the great things for both Miriam and me was, each in our own way, working through to who we really were." In their marriage, Miriam and Jeremy helped each other grow up and figure out who they were in the world—and that who they were was all right. Miriam said that accepting Jeremy's homosexuality "was all part of our acclimation to this wider world."

Jeremy added, "Miriam has a magnificent ability to shrug off the inessentials and remain concerned only with the vital center of whatever it is that's going on." And that vital center was what remained for both of them after they had gone through the difficult, sometimes painful transition following Jeremy's revelation and their divorce.

Olivia said of her ex-husband and current co-parent, "I think Mike's a nice, good, decent person—he's got a good base." She has a hard time understanding people who have children together and then part on bad terms. "At one time, you really loved this person. There was something there that made you marry this person. Why does all that have to go away?"

One of Marshall's insights grew out of his observations of others going through divorce. From his vineyards in Monterey, he commented, "I've known about some pretty long and terrible divorces. I think it has to do with the character and makeup of the people who are married. If you have a particularly bitter person to begin with, they're gonna stay that way. And depending on how much they're hurt, and how vindictive they feel, it can be a pretty nasty situation."

Muriel has had many years to think about the events that brought about the downfall of her marriage to Max. "He had a very powerful mother," she told me. "They had a definite love-hate relationship. She put Max and his brother in an orphanage when their father died, because she wanted to go on with her career. Like me, she was a painter. She was very good. They never wanted to say anything bad when she came to visit. They always said, 'Everything's fine! We're so happy to see you!'

"He tells me that if he had been who he is today when we divorced, he never would have left me. Because he realizes that a lot of the reasons we got divorced had nothing to do with me. Max left when Federico was about four; that's the same age Max was when his own father died. And I thought, knowing what he went through, how could he leave his son? He's seventy-two and his son is seven years old now. Max told me last time he was here that he feels very lucky that he's had a second chance to have a son."

Although decades younger than Muriel, Julie has also given a great deal of thought to her marriage ending just as her career as a full-time ballerina ended as well. "In retrospect," she told me, "I think that had Michael and I been more mature, and more aware of what was going on, we might have been able to find a way to be together. But I also think that the dynamic of our relationship was a problem. We both had a lot of growing up to do. When we would fight, and if Michael would storm out, I would be scared to death he was never coming back. There was a part of me that felt I wasn't good enough, that I was going to lose him. This is something in my nature that I've been working with over these years, because it's something about me, not him.

"We have less invested now," Julie continued. "We just see and accept each other as two separate human beings who have a lot of history together, and we're bound. I really see Michael more clearly. And I think he sees me more clearly."

For Molly, the divorce from Dorian allowed her to finally understand him. "Being around Bianca and Dorian, I really got to see how much of Dorian's behavior I took personally. I see how, in many ways, he's the same person he always was. Bianca just doesn't react to him in the same way I did. And I get to see, Wow! He's like that to

Bianca and that was something that always hurt my feelings—and it wasn't even about me. It was nothing personal!" It occurred to me that it would be great, in a way, if married people could see their spouses married to someone else, for just this type of insight.

Among other things, insight enables us to take a new kind of responsibility for ourselves and our feelings. As Joan wrote from Kauai, "Something that has also helped me is making myself responsible for remembering the love Ritch has for me, rather than trying to get him to say or do something loving when I feel he has treated me badly. For if there is anything I have learned over these fifteen years, it is that Ritch loves me—with all his heart, Ritch loves me. Whatever he says or does that results in my feeling angry or hurt is not because he doesn't love me. Actually, it's much more a result of the way he has so much trouble loving himself. And it's my own lack of love for myself that causes me to misinterpret him.

"And that's why we met, I think. To help each other learn to unconditionally love ourselves. If we had stayed locked in our anger and hurt, seeing the other as the enemy and cause of our pain, and burdened by the guilt of our shortcomings, we would have only reinforced the pain and fear of our unlovability. Instead, both of us, thanks to us, are better people, better lovers, better friends, better at our work, and better at living life."

If life is a process of learning to be wiser, then certainly all of these people are winning.

Samantha told me, "I really believe that Jake and I are just beginning to understand and appreciate each other as co-parents and friends. The only agenda we have is to be the best parents we can and to function in that way as a team.

"If you love and respect and value the person you married after you're no longer living as husband and wife, that's almost a purer, maybe a higher form of love. Because it's optional, really. You have a choice. You can look and see who that person really is, and you have a choice about how you feel. It's a conscious, open-eyed kind of love rather than the kind of love where you close your eyes and hope for the best.

"And now I have so much honor for Jake's decency as a human being, so much love for his devotion as a father, and so much respect for his fine qualities—his intelligence, his creativity, his many talents. I could hardly see any of this while we were still together, because both of us were so unhappy, and unhappiness really has a way of putting out the lights so that you can't see anything clearly."

Insight—about yourself, your ex, and your shared history—is your reward at the end of the rocky road. Finally, you can see clearly everything that was obscured or distorted by disappointment, hurt feelings, loneliness, rage, disgust, and fear.

It takes a lot of psychic and even physical energy to harbor such negative emotions. Letting go of them, you may be surprised at your sudden, expansive capacity to give and receive love.

CHAPTER THREE

New Spouses, New Friends

*"**W**e have this part of ourselves as human*
beings that enables us to deny what we feel,
just because we're jealous, hurt, or angry. But if
you can go below the emotion of those things,
there's something underneath: the truth of
whether or not you care for someone." — Julie

IN THE BEST of all worlds, your ex-spouse's new husband or wife is someone you really, truly like and
respect. This is, of course, especially important if
this person is going to be spending time with your
child.

I was surprised at first as stories started coming
to me over the Internet and through friends about
the profound connections forged between old
spouses and new. In my own personal circle of
acquaintances, I had known for years about the
friendship between Terry's first and second hus-

bands: how they play poker together once a month, how husband number one has done a lot of different kinds of work connected to husband number two's software company, how closely they cooperate in co-fathering the two children Terry had in her first marriage. My son Julian's pediatrician told me in passing how another patient's mother commented about her ex-husband's new wife—how she's the best thing that ever happened to him and how he's a much better father now. Someone in a dance class said that she knows someone who adores her ex-husband's new wife and claims her now as her best friend. So unless all these people are talking about the same folks, I reasoned, there seems to be something going on here—something that looks like a trend.

When I heard the story of how Julie became best friends with Michael's new wife, Lara, I was pretty impressed—especially when Julie told me how she would feel if he and Lara ever broke up. "One of my first responses would be concern for Michael," she said. "It's his second marriage, and I know how much he loves her; I just don't want him to be hurt. And Lara has become such an important part of *my* life—I don't want to lose her!

I would feel like there was something really big missing."

My feelings of amazement grew when I heard about how Bianca and Molly managed to stay best friends after trading husbands, and how twice-married Helena talks about going on a "night on the town with her husbands." I sat up and paid attention when Sybil insisted, "I've become good friends with Jonathan's lover, Bob." I wondered whether it was a fluke when Muriel said of Max's second wife, more than twenty years younger than wife number one, "Oh, yes. I really like her! I'm very good friends with Jeanette."

And then I thought, it stands to reason that your ex's new spouse may be just your cup of tea. Presumably, there were some shared interests and values that brought you and your ex together initially. It makes sense that you'd have similar taste in friends.

Personal and/or professional affinities should not really come as that much of a surprise. Adair said in speaking of her current and former husband, "Since Bill is a book editor, and Jim is a publisher, and I am a writer, we can consult with one another on projects."

Peter wrote to me, "Helena's husband and I are the best of friends. We knew each other in high school, too. He and I play a lot of sports together, and he uses me as a sounding board about relational matters at times. Their well-being in relationship is very important to me. I have an investment in it."

Peter's words were echoed by Julie's. "I've talked to Lara about this," she told me. "I have always been very protective of their relationship. When I know that she and Michael are fighting, I get a knot in my stomach. I want them to be okay. When I know they've been arguing or having a problem, I'll talk to Lara on the phone. If it seems that he's the one who's being stubborn, I'll tell Lara, 'Now give me Michael!'" Julie laughed at this. "I've said, 'Michael, you have to apologize to her! You were wrong.' Sometimes I have been able, I think, to help them hear each other. I don't ever feel like I'm butting in, because I don't butt in. But sometimes couples need help. I want so much for them both to be happy."

Franny recalled the time when she and her ex-husband, Paul, were sharing an apartment together after their divorce. "He had a girlfriend, I had a boyfriend. We did a lot of things together. I would shop for him for a birthday present for his girl-friend."

David recognizes the affinity between him and the man Susan finally married. "Candidly," he told me, "I understand him. I think if I were to look at his makeup, he's got a lot of the makeup I have."

It was Jeremy's gay friends who were able to bring a sense of reconciliation to Miriam, back when gayness wasn't something talked about openly or understood by people outside the gay community. "Some of Jeremy's friends were really helpful to me," she said. "There was a period of time when I had a terrible fear of driving. I was afraid to cross bridges. One of Jeremy's friends did a little therapy with me. He made me go through all my fears. And then I thought, 'Well, this guy isn't crazy. He's normal.' And I realized, you can be any way you want in the world, and it's okay." More than one bridge was crossed at that moment in time.

The story of Julie's ongoing relationship with Lara gives insight into the process that allowed Michael's first and second wives to become such close friends. The fact that they were both professional ballerinas provided immediate common ground. But a person with a less expansive heart than Julie's might have found this particularly hard to deal with, especially since Lara was a lot younger and reaching the height of her career while Julie, at the advanced age of twenty-nine, was retiring from the ballet stage.

When I spoke with the three of them and heard of the extreme emotional challenges of the situation, I told Julie that she has a very big heart. "It's huge!" said Lara. "Sometimes it's too big."

Lara continued, "When Michael and I were getting married, I wanted Julie to come to the wedding. We had a phone call about that, and Julie said, 'I just don't think I can.' And then, two or three years later, in one of the nicest conversations we've had, Julie said, 'I wish now that I could have come to your wedding. I wish I could have been there and seen that.'"

Julie corroborated this. "I really do wish I could have been there, because I'm their biggest fan. I always want things to be good for them. I love Lara! She's one of my best friends."

Lara explained, "I wasn't really involved in their lives when they were married. So I think it might have been easier for the two of us to get along, because I came along after all of that happened." Julie retired as a principal ballerina from Oakland Ballet in 1989. Lara joined the company that same year. Michael and Lara got married in the summer of 1992.

"Lara and I really had to work to get to know each other," said Julie, "because we didn't know each other at all. So we had a fresh start, in learning about one another."

"Julie and I have a great relationship," said Lara as the four of us sat in the living room of Michael and Lara's apartment, "because we're like other halves of each other. Julie is so sensitive and such a good, kind, caring person. It's nice to have Julie's opinion, because it makes me want to be more like her." When I commented on how articulate both she and Julie are, Lara smiled and said, "Good! We're not just bun-heads!"

"And I've learned from Lara," said Julie, "that it's good and important to be decisive sometimes, and that my emotions don't always have to rule my decisions."

Lara added, "I value Julie's opinion highly! Sometimes my too-strong personality overtakes some of my decisions, so I try and get another point of view, which is usually Julie's yang to my yin. We really complement each other!"

I responded, "You guys should have married each other!" After everyone had a good laugh over that one, Lara added, "We call each other and just bounce off each other all the time."

Like Bianca and Molly, Julie and Lara share something almost beyond the bounds of friendship in the fact that they've both been married to the same man. Such an experience seems to confer a sort of super-sisterhood on otherwise biologically unrelated women. Julie noted that this kind of friendship "doesn't just happen totally by itself. You have to have respect for the other person."

"There's implicit trust," added Lara.

Like Bianca, like Miriam—maybe like all the amicable exes in this book—Julie seems to have a remarkable ability to get to the heart of things. She cuts a path through her own negative emotions, her fears, her hurt feelings, to the emotional center, where there's only love.

"The truth is," she explained, "that I like Michael, and I like Lara. I cannot *not* like her. She's a great person. She's someone I connect with. It would be foolish to ignore that. We have this part of ourselves as human beings that enables us to deny what we feel, just because we're jealous, hurt, or angry. But if you can go below the emotion of those things, there's something underneath: the truth of whether or not you care for someone."

Julie showed me beautiful black-and-white photographs of her and Lara in a ballet that Michael had choreographed for them not long after he and Lara got married. Julie has her hand, very lovingly, around the back of Lara's neck, and Lara is supporting Julie's head as Julie is arching precariously backwards. The dance was called "Witness," and in an odd, unconscious way that all three of them acknowledged in the interviews, the dance was a metaphor for the emotional dynamic that occurred among them. In the ballet, Michael played a young boy who witnesses a woman's suicide. Julie—having left her performing career, having left her marriage to Michael—played the woman who leaps from a tall building. Lara danced the part of a spirit who guides Julie to the next plane of her existence, while Michael looks on. Even in the still photographs of the three of them dancing together, you can sense a wonderful dynamic between them—and it certainly seems extraordinary that they've all been through what they've been through. But maybe it's the depth of this experience together that has lent such depth and resonance to their dancing and choreography.

Bianca also has a lot of insight into the evolution of the friendships between her, Molly, Dorian, and Noah as they were buffeted by their storm of marital changes. "It became clear," Bianca wrote to me, "that our personalities were not the most real aspects of ourselves, even though each personality had certain qualities that seemed useful to the process. At one point early on, when I saw that Molly's feelings were understandably, deeply upset, I decided that I had to pull out of my relationship with Dorian. I thought I just needed to drop it all and make everything go back to the way it had been." This was after Molly's husband Dorian and Bianca acknowledged romantic feelings between them.

"But," Bianca continued, "it was Molly herself, with her capacity for honesty and for putting herself in other people's shoes, who told me that it wouldn't work to deny what was happening. I know she desperately needed something to change in her marriage, but I will always stand in awe of how she remained my accepting and encouraging friend in spite of the hurt feelings and the shocking turns of events. I feel the same about Noah, my dear and steadfast friend-and-husband. He took things in stride, and was able to evoke a sense of balance and calmness that supported all of us. And Dorian, who was the first to know that something was changing, had to find a deep source of courage to get through the immense trauma of being a loving father who can no longer live full-time with his children."

Part of the challenge of learning to be friends (or to be friends again) with an ex's spouse is truly seeing and hearing what is going on in a time of often turbulent emotions. Bianca reflected on this: "There were innumerable times when our thoughts and feelings, faced with so many challenging adjustments, were terrifically reactive and caught up in our personal versions of what was going on and what it meant. The worst, for me, was that Molly and I went through a phase of the 'Big Divorce' during which we were at odds and wrote many long, reactive letters projecting all kinds of things on each other. After weeks of this, I finally *heard* myself express negative judgments about her, and had the shock of realizing that what I was feeling and saying was not true, only reactive and based on my own fears. I was, shortly after that realization, immensely grateful to find myself able to apologize.

"We have since," Bianca continued, "sworn never to let ourselves pretend that we can't come to an understanding, because life has made it clear to us that the parts of us that are above the personality level are truly united. Molly and I know each other's husbands so well that we have been able to support each other particularly well with understanding giggles, shared insights, and honest observations."

Life has a way of offering us compensation for our heartaches, if only we can reach out and take it. Part of being able to love, to paraphrase what Joan said in the last chapter, is to believe that we ourselves deserve to be loved. It must be one of life's greatest emotional challenges to accept love from someone who—in another context, from another point of view—might be seen as having stolen love that is rightfully yours. Even if you're the one who initiated the divorce, your ex's new spouse or lover can be seen in this light. But if you dig deeply, and if this person is someone toward whom you'd tend to be friendly in any other situation, you might be able to see your ex's new spouse as a kind of door prize from the divorce: an ally, a friend, a new and very special member of your extended family.

So much depends on perspective. So much depends on attitude, interpretation, and mind-set. This type of friendship needs time to grow, and you and your spouse (and children, if you have them) need to take as much time as you need to heal. But it's never too late for such a friendship to suddenly blossom.

CHAPTER FOUR

Staying Amicable—Rather Than Staying Together—for the Sake of the Children

"When I was fourteen, I threatened to go down to the police station and have myself put up for adoption if my mom didn't leave my dad—things were so terrible between them, and our home was so unhappy." — Louisa

ONE OF THE MYTHS of modern life that deserves debunking is that it's a good thing to keep a bad marriage together "for the sake of the children." Unhappy marriages breed nothing but more unhappiness. Children without a good working model of a healthy love relationship between the adults in their life have a heck of a time inventing the concept from scratch when they are launched into the world beyond the confines of their family.

Olivia told me, "I don't think people should stay

together if they're unhappy. I'd rather have my son see me be very happy and set up a good role-modeling situation for a good relationship—a healthy male-female, mom-dad situation—than have him be in a house with a lot of tension and his parents living in separate rooms."

Speaking of her new partner, Olivia added, "Charlie's parents have been married over fifty years. He says they should have never stayed married, should have divorced; but his mom didn't really have anything to do and didn't know anything better. And now they're growing old together because they got to that point where, oh, what the heck! Charlie told me that he and his siblings actually prayed they'd separate or his dad would leave, because he was such an ass." Olivia continued, speaking about her own experience, "My parents divorced when I was fourteen, and after the divorce, my dad became a much better father."

The entire concept of staying together for the sake of the children is completely wrong-headed, as far as I'm concerned. "When I was fourteen," Louisa told me, "I threatened to go down to the police station and have myself put up for adoption if my mom didn't leave my dad—things were so terrible between them, and our home was so unhappy."

In contrast to "staying together for the sake of the children," I think that staying amicable for the sake of the children is a highly laudable goal. This can work if the parents are sufficiently determined, as you'll see in the stories below.

Getting There When Both Parents Are Working Toward the Same Goal

"I think if Judy and I had stayed married for a lot longer, then the marital stress could have escalated enough to affect Hannah. Since we divorced when Hannah was young and things have been so amicable, I think she grew up thinking this was sort of the natural, proper state of things. She knows she has parents who love her (including a stepmother!), and it seems to work for everyone." — Joel

Joel, the biologist from Idaho, told me his story. "Judy and I ended up moving to different places a few months after our separation. We had both become disenchanted with our respective jobs; I moved to Arizona to go to grad school and work, and Judy moved with our daughter, Hannah, to the Los Angeles area with a new job. Because of our geographical separation, I was obviously not able to take part in day-to-day parenting, but we arranged things so that Hannah and I could spend a lot of time together.

"For job reasons, Judy and her husband moved with Hannah to Canada, and Cathy [Joel's second wife] and I moved to Idaho. Because of the greater distance, we couldn't see Hannah as much. And as Hannah got older, we started flying her on her own for visits. Judy has been very accommodating and flexible, particularly with respect to being a co-parent. She has made it very easy for us to be with Hannah, either allowing Hannah to travel or permitting us to visit. Hannah has spent most of her summers and usually most of her longer school vacations with us, and Judy has never begrudged us that time."

Joel proudly continued, "Our daughter, Hannah, is an intelligent, independent, and responsible person, who is truly one of the nicest people I know. But I think if Judy and I had stayed married for a lot longer, then the marital stress could have escalated enough to affect Hannah. Since we divorced when Hannah was young and things have been so amicable, I think she grew up thinking this was sort of the natural, proper state of things. She knows she has parents who love her (including a stepmother!), and it seems to work for everyone.

"An important point for both of us was keeping a good relationship for Hannah. Hannah was less than two when Judy and I split. At first I talked about doing some sort of joint custody, but Judy was quite adamant that Hannah should have a single, full-time parent. Deep down I agreed with her, and since I felt that Judy would be very reasonable about visits, and I wanted things to be on good terms, I agreed to give her custody. We used a 'do-it-yourself' divorce kit and easily agreed to terms dividing property and setting child support. I've bent over backward never to say anything negative about Judy in front of Hannah. I suspect Judy has done the same."

Joel's is the picture-perfect story of an amicable divorce in which both parents are mature and strong enough to cooperate in ensuring the welfare of their child. When ex-spouses have not managed to progress far enough along their rocky road to healing, they have difficulty keeping things friendly—and it is the children who suffer.

Louisa's parents clearly had not reached a point of healing, and their children, unfortunately, paid a steep price for that. Louisa told me, "My dad was the big bully in our family when my parents were still together. We were all terrified of him, including my mom. After they got divorced, she took on many of the characteristics that she most hated in him. I look a lot like my dad's side of the family, and every time my mom looked at me, I guess, she saw him. Anyway, my entire adolescence seemed like a staging ground for her revenge. She was always criticizing and punishing me; nothing I did was acknowledged or appreciated—and I did a lot. I took on a lot of the mothering responsibilities for my little sister, and a lot of the cooking and so forth while my mother went back to school and then started a career. And I was a pretty good kid— I more or less stayed out of trouble, and I did well in school. But because I looked like my dad, or for whatever reasons I'll never understand, my mom was unable at that time to really like me. She'd always say how I took after my father, even when she was praising me for something—he's a pretty smart guy and he was the artist in our family—and in the next breath she'd say what a louse he was, and what a bastard.

"The awful thing was," Louisa continued, "that the same thing happened when I spent time with my dad. Somehow he sees my mom in me. And he never has anything good to say about her. They never made peace or forgave each other. They're cordial when they see each other now; and I have a pretty good relationship with both of them at this point. But it was really hell trying to grow up in that situation, both before and after the divorce. That's why I left home when I was so young."

If you're still hurting after the divorce, it can be extremely difficult to find the moral strength to deal with the pain yourself rather than putting at least some of it on your children's shoulders. I heard from someone that a child should live with the parent who speaks most highly of the other parent in a divorce. This makes a great deal of sense. Louisa said that it took her two wrong marriages and over twenty years to get over what she feels her parents did to her. "I don't blame them," she told me, "because I know that they each did what they could to be a good parent to me. People weren't as self-aware back then, and there weren't the same supports in place that you have today. Dysfunctional family situations weren't talked about on TV; they weren't talked about at all. What happened to me—and, in different ways, to my brother and sister—was simply fallout. It wasn't because my parents are bad or didn't love us. It was just that their pain was too much for them, and they didn't get any help from the outside. I know that if they had it all to do over again, they would never do what they did back then."

Bianca, Dorian, Molly, and Noah are part of a completely different era. While they definitely pursued their own happiness in "The Big Divorce," they did so with eyes open at every step of the way, and with their ears keenly attuned to the emotional needs of Dorian and Molly's two children, Flynn and Caitlin.

Dorian told me, "I was living with Molly and having a very hard time, and yet this woman is the best mother that these kids could ever have. And I'm a good dad. I'm unwilling to sacrifice my life for the kids because I believe that what you do with your life is what you teach your kids. And if

I live my life under a rock, I'm saying, 'Oh, kids—this is how you live your life. You live it under a rock. You don't follow your feelings, you don't try to do the best that you can do.' What we're showing our kids is, 'Wow! You really have to go for what you believe in, you really need to stand up for love, you need to go for fulfilling your life in a true and loving way.'

"We both wanted to do that," Dorian went on. "I'm not even sure what the process is that people go through when they just go into that place other than love. They don't see the other person for who they are."

Molly added, "They don't honor each other's role as parents. That honoring—I think we've all done that, Noah included. I've heard the kids talking to their friends at school and they'll say, 'We have two dads!' Or 'two moms!' They really consider all of us their parents."

"As far as my role as step-parent," said Bianca, "one of the most crucial things has been Molly's willingness to trust me with the kids. I can't recall her ever expressing concern about my fledgling mothering skills. Do you see what a difference that makes? I've been able to find my own way to relate to the kids without the dread of being observed skeptically or critically, without feeling like I have to compare myself to her all the time. Of course, I've often thought, 'Now, would Molly approve of how I handled that?' But all along she's given me a vote of confidence, even made it clear she thinks it's good for the kids to have a second mom who does things and sees things a little differently. So did Dorian, for me and for Noah, and I'm so glad he and Molly have been so wise about this. It could have been so miserable if Noah and I had become step-parents in an atmosphere of mistrust and scrutiny. We're all just trying to do our best with what we've got."

Molly told me, "Many are amazed at the level of participation and trust that Bianca and I share in each other's lives. But Bianca is a wonderful complement and counterpoint to my mothering style, and I'm grateful that my kids have her influence and friendship. I've tried to actively 'make room' for her to have her own relationship with them. For her part, Bianca has honored my role as their biological mother, with all its inherent considerations, and has acted in a spirit of support. We often put our heads together to figure out how to best work with whatever issues come up in the kids' lives. The children have never felt like they had to choose at anyone's expense."

For Colin, the British-born television producer, there was never any question about making his divorce amicable. "Our kids love us both," he wrote to me, "and understand us perfectly (or as well as any kids can understand their parents). Our now-grown children have four parents instead of two, because both of us, with new and loving companions, bring new values to the family situation. Our granddaughters feel this, too, and love all their six grandparents devotedly. Remember, too, that once we were able to disengage, my ex and I spared our children any further pain. The kids were able to sense immediately that the disengagement was gentle, loving, and supportive—so if they are ever in a similar situation, they have role models, I hope."

Josie wrote to me from England, "It would be dishonest of me to say that I do not grieve for the loss of family that divorce brings. No child would ever wish his or her parents to be divorced, either. Whatever went wrong with our marriage, it was not about the children, and I think that the four-some we were was always very strong. But having acknowledged that, there are many very positive aspects of our current situation that bring great pleasure. I have been able to establish a different kind of relationship with both my children, which is in many ways a better relationship for me as an individual than it might have been if Noël and I were together.

"Even though I am in a very strong relationship now," Josie added, "I am a much more separate and independent person than I was in the early years of my marriage. It's sometimes harder to see your parents as separate people if they have always been together. Perhaps I provide a better role model for my daughters as a more independent person than as a mother/wife. I have always worked; but for most of the period of my marriage, I worked from home and, counter to expectations, that probably made my work less rather than more visible.

"Both my daughters have also formed a very good relationship with my second partner. He is very different from Noël, and that has perhaps helped; but they both seem to be very fond of him, and he reciprocates that feeling. Does this make my daughters' lives better? I don't know, but I hope it has added something for them."

From his home in Bethesda, Peter e-mailed me, "Helena and I continue to talk about and share support of our only son, who is now a college student. We had to do a lot of forgiving, and we were able to do that, in part, due to our long history of connection, as well as our commitment to our son's welfare."

In a separate communication, Helena told me, "We have been able to renegotiate our shared vision and goals for our son, and most of the time present a 'united' front. More importantly, he has seen that we care for each other very much, despite the turmoil of the end of the marriage and the initial stages of the divorce. Although our son is an adult, living on his own, I am sure that it is gratifying for him to know that his parents like each other, care for each other, and always will."

Adair, a writer and columnist for the *San Francisco Chronicle*, wrote to me, "I've heard that fewer than ten percent of couples get along well enough to make joint custody work. Jim and I are either having trouble getting in touch with our anger, or we are just plain lucky."

Adair's first husband started out as her English teacher at the College of Marin. "In time, we got married and he flirted with babies over my shoulder in coffee shops. We had our own—a boy and a girl, one year apart—a lot else happened, and now our increasingly complex story revolves around them. It's extremely rare for either child to come home and find none of their three parents at home. One of us is always available. After six years of separation, I still try to impress the kids with how lucky they are, having both parents so near when their friends' fathers live in L.A. or New York. They don't feel especially lucky, but they're getting closer to accepting it now. Another couple hundred years should do it."

Franny and Paul pulled off an unbelievably amicable divorce over twenty years ago, after a marriage that lasted almost as long. Franny told me over the phone, "I can't understand people who get divorced and hate each other—especially if they have children."

Sybil told me, "Jenny is only seven, and she really doesn't understand the sexuality thing. Everybody loves her, and so she's happy with that. But I think she believes that Bob and Jonathan are roommates and sleep together because they have to. She's said, 'I want Daddy to get a bigger place.

Then I can have my own room, and Bob can have his own room, and Daddy can have his own room.'

"Jonathan travels a lot, so Jenny's with me about ninety percent of the time; but we have a very flexible custody agreement, which I find is really preferable to anything else. So if Jonathan's in town, I'm happy for her to be with him, and she wants to be with him, and he's happy to do that. Our daughter is one of the main reasons why we do what we do. You have to be strong, and it helps you focus. It's such a wonderful experience to be a parent. It's all worth it, whatever we've been through."

Olivia told me, "Very early on, Mike and I made the decision to separate our issues and to keep them as separate as possible from the health and well-being of our son. We were both very clear about that. No matter what went on between us, that was completely separate, and no matter what interactions we had or what decisions we had to make, Zachary would always come first. Always. I'm grateful Mike can be as reasonable about this whole thing as he's been, and that he helped make the transition okay. People who use their relationship problems against their children, or involve their children in it—I just can't understand how they can do it.

"I look at Zachary's situation, and I think Zach is really lucky to have Mike and Charlie in his life," Olivia continued. "I mean, a lot of kids don't have that. I don't think people should stay together if they're unhappy. If you have children, you try your best to stay together—but sometimes you can't."

As you'll read in the next section, the presence of children can sometimes lend clarity to even the most painful decisions.

Painful Decisions

"It's not a rational response. You know they're miserable. You know you're all miserable in the situation as it is. But there's something so final about divorce." — Louisa

One of the hardest things to capture when you're in the throes of divorce is a sense of perspective. Your strong feelings, as well as your ex's strong feelings, are bound to give you a very different view of the same situation. When it comes to explaining your situation to your child, he or she is left with the task of constructing a complete and truthful picture from these differing and often competing points of view.

I interviewed Charlotte, a bright and articulate twelve-year-old whose father and mother split up when she was four, just months after Charlotte underwent life-threatening surgery for a congenital heart defect. Her parents, Ellen and Ernie, were both social workers and child advocates by profession. Both were meticulous and conscientious in giving Charlotte, then four, as much solid information as they felt she could handle and as much reassurance as possible.

When I asked Charlotte how she would advise two parents contemplating a divorce, she didn't hesitate for a moment in answering me. "Be sure to be honest with your children about what's happening. Tell your kid everything that's happening with the divorce, and tell it honestly. Don't tell it how you see it, but how it really is. Don't tell it from your point of view. Like, oh, it's all your dad's fault, or, oh, it's all your mother's fault. Make sure it's an honest explanation of why you two are breaking up, and be sure and tell them that it's not their fault. Tell it to them straight. Just be real with them about what's happening and why. Because, more often than not, kids will want to know what's happening."

Children, on some level, always want their parents to stay together, no matter how bad the marriage is. Louisa told me, "Even though I was the one who was probably urging my mom the most to leave my dad, there was still part of me that hated to see even the hope of being a happy, united family dashed forever when they got their divorce. It's not a rational response. You know they're miserable. You know you're all miserable in the situation as it is. But there's something so final about divorce.

"And maybe because I lobbied so strongly for it, I felt a little guilty when it finally happened. Kids don't want to feel they have that kind of power—that they're the ones in control rather than the adults. My mom says I'm nuts—that her decision had nothing to do with anything I said. But I don't think that's true. I think I gave her just that little push she needed to go through with it." Louisa paused, then continued, "The thing is that even if the situation you're in is terrible, there's no assurance that any change you make won't be even worse. So it was scary for all of us, I think. No one felt in control. No one knew what was going to happen to us or whether we were even a family anymore."

Charlotte's mother, Ellen, is still processing her feelings about Ernie, who was diagnosed with a terminal, inoperable illness shortly after their divorce. For a long time after he died, she didn't know whether to consider herself a widow or a divorcée. She was both, in a sense, because the two traumatic events occurred in such close sequence. Co-parenting is a learning process—just like parenting within a marriage—which evolves over time. And Ellen's time with Ernie as a co-parent was cut short.

"As a father," Ellen told me, "Ernie was Mr. Mellow. We used to laugh about how differently we approached parenthood. If I was 'on duty,' I would make fresh organic baby foods in the blender; he would give Charlotte whatever was closest to the front of the fridge—when I'd ask him what he'd fed her, his standard reply was 'beer and pepperoni sticks' (two of his favorite foods). Charlotte was crazy about her daddy. He was funny and allowed her to do almost anything that wouldn't interfere with his work."

Charlotte told me that her mother tried very hard to keep their family together. "The divorce wasn't her idea, and it wasn't one of those bitter divorces—like they broke up because they were fighting. I never saw or heard my parents fight, my whole life. Dad just didn't want to be a husband. He didn't think he was ready for marriage. So he moved out. And shortly before he died, they got a divorce. They were separated for about four years."

"One thing that we both agreed upon," Ellen wrote to me, "was the imperative of continuing to do shared, pleasurable activities together with Charlotte as she healed. About a month after Ernie moved to his own place, we made a visit to Fairyland, where we ran into a mutual friend. She said to me, 'Oh, I'm so glad to see that your marriage has held up under all the pressure'—referring to Charlotte's illness. I turned to Ernie and said how uncomfortable her comment had made me. His response was to shrug his shoulders and say, 'I think she's right; look how much happier we all seem now.' Since, inside, I really didn't feel happy, it felt very phony to me to come across as if everything was copacetic.

"We continued to celebrate holidays, attend work-related and social engagements together, and even went to therapy (we joked about what to call it: 'post-marital counseling,' 'growing pain therapy,' 'co-parenting counseling') for almost two years together. His attitude towards fifty-fifty custody was, typically, like it was no biggie—Mom's car, Dad's car, Mom's house, Dad's house—what's the difference? Although he was very flexible around how the fifty-fifty thing was worked out, he was very clear about the exact split. It was extremely important to him that no one ever feel that he reneged on his responsibilities as a co-parent just because he didn't feel like being married anymore. The only time he ever wavered on fifty-fifty was right after the Loma Prieta earthquake, when he (much to my surprise) brought Charlotte over here because he thought we all needed to be together. Also, during the '91 Oakland Hills fire, when he had to evacuate, he allowed her to spend a few extra days here.

"When Ernie became ill," Ellen continued, "the fifty-fifty arrangement became even more important to him. I allowed Charlotte to spend as much time with him as he was physically capable of handling, up until the day he died. He wrote her a letter about a week before his death, when he could barely hold a pencil, professing his love and his great joy for the chance to know her, and his confidence that she would remain a remarkable force in the lives of all of us lucky enough to be a part of her life. He also wrote, 'The divorce was never your mom's idea; I was just too weird to stay married to her. Don't ever blame her for this fact, and always remember how lucky you are to have her for a mom.'

"Today, Charlotte talks about the shared custody in very negative terms—'no one asked me what I wanted.' So, even with all of our collective efforts to support her and to change rather than disintegrate our family life, her retained experience is of feeling 'like a ping-pong ball' and hating the back-and-forth two-house schlep."

This may be what Charlotte tells her mother when she's feeling angry or frustrated. But the twelve-year-old put a somewhat different message across when she spoke, in private, to me. "I was really lucky," she told me while munching on some sausages—and I couldn't help but remember those spicy snacks Ernie prepared for Charlotte when she was a little girl. "I got to see both my parents a lot. But every night, when I switched houses, I would always cry myself to sleep. It was really painful."

Molly and Dorian's youngest child, Caitlin, also had a hard time in the first year or so, especially on the first night of every new week when she and her brother went from their Mom's to their Dad's or back again. But Caitlin, now nine, is a wondrously bright, creative, and well-adjusted child, as is her brother, Flynn.

It seems awfully important for parents operating from separate households to remember that all children—whether or not their family is under one roof—are unhappy sometimes. There's no way to make childhood pain-free. All we can do as parents—whether married, separated or divorced—is to give unstintingly of our love, be the best parents we can be, and work as much as possible as a team, whether or not we live in the same house.

"When I was smaller," Charlotte told me, "I thought maybe my parents' separation had something to do with me, but both of them assured me, 'No, no—it had nothing to do with you. We both still love you very, very much.' And now I know that's true. It wasn't my fault. Dad just wasn't cut out to be a married man." Then she added, "A kid really needs both parents to grow up right. I mean, I haven't had my dad for six years, but at least I had him for those first six years. He really loved me. A lot of the kids I know, their parents are separated or divorced. I would say it's about fifty-fifty. They seem completely normal. They have happy childhoods. My friend can sometimes seem a little depressed—but her parents are together."

Charlotte's mother, Ellen, works with abused, neglected, or abandoned children at the Center for the Vulnerable Child at Children's Hospital in Oakland. When I confided to her my fears that my son Julian might end up feeling like a ping-pong ball in his back-and-forth routine between his two homes, she sent me words of comfort by e-mail. "Being who I am, added to the situations I confront daily in my work life, forces me to think of positive spins for just about everything, in order to keep from cracking up. Although I, too, have been profoundly shaken by Charlotte's expressions of anguish over all the things she's had no control of in her life, I also feel that she has developed such remarkable resilience, and (if I may toot my own horn a tad...) has had a golden opportunity to observe my learning and coping process.

"This has to pay off, in ways I can only imagine, for her and all the other little ones who shoulder the burdens of their parents' eccentricities and decisions over the years. When I turned forty-six last summer, I asked Charlotte what she thought she would remember about me when she turned forty-six. Her answer reinforced my comment about enhancing resilience. She said, 'I think most of all that I will remember that my mom loved to laugh.' If, after everything we have been through, this is her primary perception, we have done well."

There are so many things we can't control. Short of heroics unavailable to most of us outside the medical profession, we can't keep anyone else from dying. We can do our best to live in a healthy way, but we have no real control over the accidents or diseases that can send us or a loved one to an early grave. We can try to keep love alive in our marriage—we can try hard. But even the greatest effort may fall short of saving a marriage if the glue that holds it together has dried up or run out.

We have no control over our ex-spouse's behavior. We can only hope to influence it positively through our own compassionate and forgiving attitude—with love, respect, and honor. We can only hang on to our sense of humor and hope for the best.

The nicer you are to your ex (unless your ex is really psychotic or in the throes of substance abuse), the better it will be for your children. The equation is a very simple one. Children suffer less from divorce if their parents get along well. It's ideal for the children if their parents are friends.

Jason, at thirty, is a successful construction manager in San Francisco. His parents, Jeremy and Miriam, separated when Jason was four. They had been friends since childhood, and they remained the closest of friends following their divorce, after Jeremy realized that he was gay.

Jason told me: "I feel very fortunate that my parents saw each other on a fairly regular basis and were friendly and got along just fine. It was normal to me, but at some point I realized that it was not the norm. Other kids' parents fought or didn't get along or used the kids as means of fighting or what have you. I just realized I was very fortunate to find myself in the position I was in."

Jason understands that his father's sexual orientation made the marriage untenable. His parents' breakup makes sense to him. "I think it was a great benefit. I can only imagine what it would have been like if my parents had stayed together and forced themselves to be miserable on my behalf. I'm sure they told you they have a long history together. They go back so far, it's almost like there was no other option. I mean, how could they let all that go away?

"I'm currently working with my dad," Jason told me. Jeremy is an award-winning architect known for his bold and unusual designs. He and Jason have been developing a building project together. "I've been close to both of them over the years. Obviously I was much closer to my mother as I grew up and was into high school. She and my step-father were my primary parental group. My father was always around, and I still saw him on a fairly regular basis. I consider myself to have two fathers, really. I don't feel cheated at all. Lee [Miriam's second husband] came in when I was pretty young, and we had a couple of talks early on, where he wanted to be my friend and try not to get between me and my father—he made that very clear. At the same time, he took on a few of those paternal responsibilities and I'm thankful that he did, because the influence was good to have. It was sort of a trade-off. I would spend time with my dad, and with Lee and my mother as well.

"To this day, I tell my friends I'm going to go up to my mother's house, and my father and my step-father will be there. And people say to me, 'Both of them will be there?!' You know, they trip on that—can't believe it. They always say, 'You're so lucky!' You learn lots of things from parents, both verbally and nonverbally. There was a lot of communication and a lot of openness and honesty about things that I took away from all of this."

In my own situation, I feel heartened by Jason's comments. Like any parent, I want so much for things to turn out well for my child. I want to do right by him. I know that there's an abundance of love in his life, and I can only hope that this will prepare the ground for a future in which he's adept both at giving and receiving love.

"Wanting to provide a model for healthy love between a man and a woman," Samantha told me, "was truly one of the reasons why I opted out of my marriage. Our daughter wasn't going to learn about this from me and Jake. Jake's depression had sucked the love right out of our marriage. Staying amicable—rather than staying together—was the biggest favor I felt we could do for our child, for her future as a loving and caring human being with strong attachments to other loving and caring people. And, of course, I made the decision out of concern for my own happiness or lack thereof. Someone told me that a happy mother makes a happy family, and I really believe it's true—a happy mother and a happy father, whether or not they stay married."

Breaking up a family is always a painful decision—and the pain of being a broken family on some level never goes away. It's like the wound that doesn't heal that Molly talked about. And yet, as painful as it may sometimes be, the wound is a battle scar, a testimonial to your courage to try to make your life--and your children's lives—better in the long term.

CHAPTER FIVE

In-Laws and Out-Laws

*"**I** call Michael's parents my 'out-laws.'
When I run into his parents at the grocery
store, we hug in the aisles." — Julie*

THERE'S NO DOUBT that divorce entails loss—loss of
your intact nuclear family, loss of a certain dream
of what family life is supposed to look like.
Divorce dashes to smithereens the expectations
you had when you got married.

The question is, what do you do with the pieces
of your broken dream?

The amicable exes I interviewed for this book
consciously and with determination took those
pieces and made a beautiful new mosaic out of
them. In many cases, this mosaic includes most or
all of the elements that were part of their extended
family picture as a married person. Beloved in-laws
were given places of honor in their newly recon-

figured family constellation. New places were made for their ex-spouse's new husband or wife. Step-children were welcomed in. New boundaries were drawn. But there was still part of the overall picture that could only be filled by their ex-spouse—and so they mortared in this section of the mosaic with special care and an eye for detail.

Some of the exes opted, no doubt politely, to exclude certain people from the picture. When you get married, you simply open a door and watch the new relatives and family connections troop inside your living room with their muddy shoes. When you're reconfiguring your new extended family after divorce, everyone who enters has to have a ticket—and you're the person issuing the tickets. Did your mother-in-law always hate your guts? "I'm so sorry, Ma'am. This show is all sold out," you say, smiling your most apologetic smile. Did you dread the Sunday dinners at your sister-in-law's? Guess what? You don't have to go anymore if you don't want to—although you may want to send your kids with your ex while you go to your samba class.

Were your spouse's parents the mom and dad you always wanted, and does the thought of being exiled or replaced in their affections simply wrench your insides? Good news—you don't have to lose them. Read the stories that follow, and take heart!

Claudine, a physician, is married to Noël, head of a New York think tank, who was formerly married to Josie. "Noël has one of the most amazing ex-situations I know," Claudine wrote to me. "Josie stays with us when she's in New York. We dine *chez elle* when we're in England. In March, we'll attend her parents' fifty-fifth wedding anniversary. We were invited to—and attended—the fiftieth as well. At the fiftieth, I asked Josie's parents if, given how much Noël loves them and how much I had come to care for them, they would be willing to be honorary grandparents for our daughters. Delighted is not the word! It was very emotional."

Josie wrote to me from England about her relationship with Noël's new family. "Noël has told you about my trip to New York two years ago, which I too enjoyed very much. It was very generous of Claudine to be so open and hospitable, too, and I was pleased to get to know his new daughters, who are a very important part of my own daughters' family, and thus of my extended family."

Peter and Helena, both epidemiologists, were married long enough to raise a son together. Peter wrote to me by e-mail, "For years after my divorce, whenever I went to New York, I would stay with Helena's mother. We would sit around and have the most marvelous conversations about life. She was a wonderful woman, whom I admired greatly. I flew out for her funeral, and we were all together to lend comfort due to that very great loss. Helena and I have both stayed fairly close to each other's extended families, writing, visiting, calling. I once went to Minneapolis to see a new, 'prospective' woman, and stayed with one of Helena's maternal great-aunts, who gave me advice."

Why throw out anything good that you can salvage from the marital bond? The amicable exes in this book may seem like a particularly forgiving lot, but I truly believe that practicality rather than saintliness is one of the common attributes among them. They know a good thing when they have it, and they were bound and determined not to lose it just because their marriage was falling apart.

Adair, who lives with her new husband in the same duplex with Jim, her former husband and the father of her children, is a stellar example of practicality coupled with good nature. "Jim is still invited to celebrations with my family, and frequently comes. Once he invited my whole family to Thanksgiving—and I have six brothers and sisters. I don't see his family, but then they live in South Dakota. The kids go visit them."

Mimi, who is now in her seventies, is still friendly with her ex-husband's children from his first marriage. "He was married and had two children," she explained to me, "then I had two children with him. His son, my step-son, when we got married, was ten years old and he lived with us. We never stopped being a family."

Ellen wrote to me about her continued connection to her late ex-husband Ernie's family after their divorce: "One piece of the past that has stuck with me is the way in which Ernie's family almost ignored the divorce and maintained a very close bond with me and our daughter, Charlotte. When Shirley—Ernie's mom, who lives in Idaho—introduces me to friends, cousins, or others, she never describes me as an 'ex' anything but as her daughter-in-law. While this might strike some people as a little weird, it makes sense to me. She never accepted Ernie's need to be un-married.

"I am very close to his family and have been all along," Ellen continued. "They are wonderful, warm, loving people. Charlotte spends at least a couple of weeks with her Idaho family every summer, and we have Thanksgiving, most years, with them. I have an annual trek to the cabin on the Salmon River with Ernie's sister, Chris, where we lie on the hammock, drink lots of beer and laugh, cry, and analyze the past, present, and future. I know that his family greatly respects the job I have done (and am doing) raising Charlotte, and they are all crazy about her. Ernie's paternal grandma was the school librarian in their little Idaho town for thirtysome-odd years. The fact that Charlotte is such a bookaholic brings her endless joy. The two of them spend hours going through Grandma's enormous collection of books, magazines, and journals. When Charlotte had her third surgery (about a year and a half after Ernie's death), Grandma came and stayed with us for a few weeks. Unfortunately, she does not travel well and has not come to visit us here since that time. But we talk on the phone often, and certainly I think of them as 'my' family."

Sybil and Jonathan's daughter, Jenny, is eight

years old now. "I have to say," Sybil told me, her brown eyes wide with wonder, "that my parents, who are in their seventies, have been great. My daughter usually spends the summers with my parents in North Carolina. Jonathan has an office in New York. He spends about half his time there, and he likes to take Jenny occasionally. He wanted to take her this summer and knew that he was going to have to do some work, so he invited my mother. So my mother flew to New York and stayed with my gay ex-husband and my daughter in a loft in Manhattan for a week. They did touristy things during the day and went out to dinner at night, and they all had a blast."

Sybil is still hurting from her loss of Jonathan-as-husband, but she has a lively appreciation for Jonathan-as-friend. She has also become close friends with Jonathan's lover, Bob, who often babysits for Jenny and attends special events at her school. At one such event that Bob attended when Jonathan was out of town, Sybil was sure that a lot of people mistook Bob for her date. Jonathan had arranged in secret for Bob to pick out a Mother's Day present there for Sybil. "Jonathan is very generous," she told me.

"Jonathan's parents are younger than my parents—they're just in their sixties. They still work. They're in Seattle, and they have actually had a really hard time with Jonathan's sexuality. About two years ago, I called his mother and said, 'I really want to bring Jenny up to see you.' I knew if I didn't do it, it wasn't going to happen.

"At first she seemed taken aback. But I went up, and we had a wonderful time. She's kind of a to-the-point person, and as we were getting ready to leave, she said, 'How much were your tickets?' And I was, like, 'Excuse me?' 'How much were your plane tickets? We want to pay for them.' And so once or twice a year they fly Jenny and me up to see them."

Sybil smiled as she continued, "We have a wonderful relationship. The last time we were up there, she introduced me to someone as her daughter-in-law. Afterward she said, 'I hope you don't mind. You know, you'll always be our daughter-in-law.' Jonathan has two sisters I'm very close to. And Jenny has cousins. When we see them, it's great—but we don't get to see them enough, because they don't live nearby.

"My parents and Jonathan's parents love each

other," Sybil went on, "but because they're on opposite coasts, they don't get to see each other that often. But in 1991 Jonathan and I gave my parents a fortieth wedding anniversary party. Jonathan's parents flew to North Carolina for the party; then they basically couldn't wait to get rid of Jonathan and me so that the four of them—Jonathan's parents and my parents—could go off on a trip. My parents have a mountain house, and they were going to vacation there together. They all get along great."

Miriam and her ex-husband Jeremy went through a situation that was similar to Sybil and Jonathan's, but they went through it almost twenty years earlier, when such things were not so readily accepted or well defined. Miriam's father, a minister in South Dakota, had always thundered from the pulpit about homosexuality being "an abomination." There wasn't much support from the couple's families of origin, with the exception of one of Miriam's sisters. But Miriam's new family warmly embraced Jeremy, who is the most charming of men, as a wonderful new part of their lives. Miriam told me, "Lee refers to my ex-husband Jeremy as his 'husband-in-law.'"

Whenever her seventy-two-year-old ex-husband Max is in town with his wife and seven-year-old child, Muriel, who loves children, often babysits for little Sasha. When people stop them to chat, they always assume he's her grandson, and Muriel doesn't bother explaining.

There's no word in our language for Sasha's familial relationship to Muriel. "Sasha is brilliant and sweet and he's so much like Federico," she told me, referring to her son, who is now a successful CEO in his mid-thirties. "Like Max says, Sasha has Federico's mannerisms. Just the way he is reminds us both of the way Federico was as a little boy. Federico loves his little half-brother, who's a little jealous of Federico's three-year-old daughter. Sasha absolutely adores Federico, and won't let go of him when he's around. He just clings to him.

"Max's wife asked Federico if he'd be kind of a surrogate father for Sasha. She wanted him to be there for Sasha and to do all the things with Sasha that Max probably won't be able to do—like take him camping and climbing, doing all these outdoor activities. He's definitely not a surrogate father, but Federico is extremely involved with

Sasha. I have this photograph of them, and Sasha looks like Federico's son."

In a sense, this hearkens back to the days when people had very large families, and the eldest child was indeed very much like a parent to the younger ones. We are perhaps, in the first moments of the twenty-first century, rediscovering everything that's good about belonging to a tribe.

Julie, the ballerina, was close to Michael's parents while they were married and has stayed close to them after their divorce. She's delighted and grateful that her extended family got wider and even more wonderful when Michael married Lara. "I consider Michael—and Lara—to be my family," she told me emphatically. "We're all born into our families, and then we create our families, too. We were family once, and we remain family.

"Lara's parents are wonderful, too. Sometimes I even talk to her mom on the phone." Lara's parents welcomed Julie into the family when Michael and Lara got married. "I just felt totally—" Julie hesitated for a beat, searching for the right words, "like a step-daughter.

"I call Michael's parents my 'out-laws.' When I run into his parents at the grocery store, we hug in the aisles. A few months ago, his mom needed some dental work, and Michael and Lara were going to be out of town. So I took her to her appointments. She introduced me to the dentist as her daughter-in-law. Of course, I'm not anymore—there's a different daughter-in-law. But it makes me feel good that she still thinks of me as family."

Julie told me, "Michael and Lara come to family dinners with my family occasionally, and we almost always spend holidays together."

"And my mom," said Lara, "went to Julie's dad's house for dinner once. They're really friendly."

There's a word in Yiddish that defines the relationship between the two mothers of a married couple—each is a *mechutonesteh* to the other (fathers are *mechutonim*). Is there a word in any language for the relationship between the parents of ex-spouses? Obviously, it's time to add some new words to the sociological lexicon.

"We work together, we play together, and we love each other!" Lara told me. "I think it's still an uncomfortable situation for most people, because the majority of people are not like we are."

But there are some other pioneers out there.

While Molly was married to Dorian, both his

mother and his step-mother became beloved mentors and friends to Molly. "That was another part of my grief," she explained. "I knew that Dorian and I had just separated. But what about my relationship with them? These women became my mothers. Dorian's mother supported me through childbirth. She was always a really strong presence in mothering and parenting for both of us. I really bonded with his mothers."

When Molly's best friend Bianca married Dorian, and Molly married Bianca's ex-husband Noah, the quartet encountered a bit of disbelief and resistance from their in-laws and out-laws— but not for long. "Early on," said Molly, "I tried to make room, because I knew Bianca needed to take her place as the daughter-in-law in the family. But Dorian's parents made it really clear to me that I still had a place there." Molly paused for a moment. "They were really open-hearted about it. They embraced Bianca; and I stand in their eyes, because I'm the mother of Dorian's children, as a daughter-in-law still."

Bianca chimed in, "It's not just because she's the mother of Dorian's children! They know her and love her."

"They've been very embracing of *me*!" said Noah. "They're just really gracious."

Dorian's parents divorced when he was twenty-four; both made new marriages. "My parents separated very negatively," he told me. "*Her* parents," he said, pointing to Bianca, "separated very negatively. *Her* parents," he added, pointing to Molly, "separated very negatively. I have these impressions of my mom and dad all of a sudden hating each other, and I'm like, this doesn't make sense to me! And I imagine it's the same for Bianca and Molly also."

Dorian and Bianca, Noah and Molly chose different paths than those their parents took, even though they passed through the same territory of marital difficulty and change.

These are all stories of turning losses into gains, and perhaps of making lemons into lemonade. Certainly the property settlement, as we know it, is far too limited in what it covers. Why haggle over who gets the stereo when such nurturing, life-sustaining relationships are at stake? What do we have that is more precious than our most positive family connections? Why do we assume that half of these must be the casualty of any divorce?

If a divorce ritual ever becomes standard in our

culture, it should certainly include a pledge by all concerned members of each extended family to honor in divorce the ties that bound them together in marriage. Divorce needs to be focused more precisely on the conjugal separation of the husband and wife, who are each going their separate romantic way. Just as the divorcing pair doesn't need to dump their friendship along with their marriage, the entire family portrait needn't be torn in half. In fact, it's a downright shame and a waste to do so.

You can invite whomever you please into the post-divorce era of your life: in-laws, out-laws, and all your friends. It's a great big airplane you're piloting, with lots of seats—and you can take whom you want with you, given that they're not afraid of flying. Hold tight to your loved ones and enjoy the ride!

CHAPTER SIX

It Takes a Village to Make a Family

*"**T**hanksgiving at our house is a very special event—usually not just my ex, but my husband's ex and her current husband attend. They all contribute delicious family recipes. The children—ours, his, hers—all benefit from our ability to create such a warm and fun holiday event on a regular basis. It's something that we all look forward to every year." — Helena*

I DON'T KNOW what gave anyone the notion that the nuclear family was a good idea. Apart from Ward and June Cleaver, I think that precious few husbands and wives in the wildly sentimentalized fifties were actually happy (and Ward and June were only virtually happy in their fictive television realm). Dads hardly spent any time with their kids. Work for them was often meaningless and oppressive, but it provided an escape from the excessive emotional burdens of family life. Moms spent too much time with their kids, without respite, often turning to prescription drugs and alcohol for solace. Maybe the kids were the only ones who were having a good time—that is, if the parents were good at keeping their misery under wraps.

Personally, I didn't think it was any fun at all, and my childhood contained only negative lessons about how to live a spiritually and emotionally rich and rewarding life. I looked at my parents, shook my head, and vowed to myself, "Well, I know I won't do it that way, at least!"

Our culture is odd in that we're expected as parents and home-dwellers to do so very much all on our own, in an emotional vacuum, and with precious little help or advice. We get inundated with gadgets and crockery when we get married—people simply throw expensive presents our way. But there's absolutely no one there when the honeymoon's over to help you figure out how to run a household, or how to nurse a baby (short of La Leche League), or how to negotiate the division of household chores. Every nuclear family has to discover these things anew for themselves in an endless, boring, often infuriatingly stressful process of reinventing the wheel.

Hillary's right: it does take a village to raise a child, and it takes a village to make a family as well. Maybe because the exes in this book already saw themselves as trailblazers in bucking the stereotype of the bitter and divisive divorce, they have felt freer than others might to forge broader tribal bonds beyond the confines of their immediate family. As far as I can tell, everyone involved has benefited from the nurturing energy of this extended sense of community.

The village motif becomes particularly compelling when tragedy strikes a family. Ellen wrote to me, "When Ernie was diagnosed with terminal, inoperable cancer soon after our divorce, all our earlier issues seemed so petty. I felt guilty that I had any lingering negative feelings about our strange permutation of family life. The need to make critical, immediate decisions about so many things brought us quickly back into a very intimate space. He and I seemed to adapt to this sobering reality better than any of our friends or family members. We briefly entertained the idea of Ernie moving back into our home; for many reasons, we decided that maintaining separate households would be better for everyone.

"Members of Ernie's family came down from Idaho and moved in with him, and we reconfigured into an expanded support team focused on helping him conquer his disease. I became an important player in the maintenance of his whole family's sanity during this very difficult time. I took his mom, for example, to the hairdresser once a week; switched cars with his dad, who couldn't fit into Ernie's little sports car; took his sister (whom I have always loved and admired) out for lunch; found an M.D. who would help to find alternative pain and cancer treatment options, and so on. The 'divorce' seemed like it almost melted away beneath all the other compelling issues."

Ellen continued, "I remember, after Ernie died (some eight months after his diagnosis), joining a dating service, and, without even realizing it, checking off under marital status both 'widowed' and 'divorced,' which required some creative explanations to those brave enough to respond!"

Dorian, who co-parents his two children with his wife, his ex-wife, and his wife's ex-husband, told me, "When children live with their two biological parents, the father gives a heavy-duty dose of, 'This is my reality and this is what the world looks like.'

The mother does the same. And it can be smothering to the kids. As soon as they get old enough to have any sense of their own about who they are and what their own reality is, they have to just push aside their parents. And there's this gap there that needs to be worked with. But in our situation (Dorian's two children split their time between their father and step-mother and their mother and step-father) there hasn't been this dominant paradigm in their life: 'This is how it is.' They're always coming into another situation."

Noah, the children's step-father, added, "They have four views of how it is, and none of them is oppressive, I think."

"The children aren't having to throw off anything," said Dorian. "It's safe for them to develop their own inherent, natural relationship to life without having any covering over it."

"That's the village," said Molly, the children's biological mother. "I think that's what people are talking about."

"And so here's our village," said Dorian. "We have four loving parents supporting the kids. In a marriage, when there's a divorce, usually it goes from two to one. This went from two to four."

"They're so lucky," said Molly, who is aware, as all four of the adults are, of the unusual nature of their situation, "because none of us had to go through just losing our spouse or being left. The children have always known Bianca and Noah—they've always been fixtures in our households. Flynn used to go up and stay with Bianca and Noah in the country. Bianca stayed a couple of days a week in our house in Berkeley, and attended Caitlin's home birth. It was kind of magical. We were able to just tell the children that our family was going to be bigger."

Part of the joy of having an amicable arrangement with your ex-spouse is that holidays can still be joyful and inclusive. "We spend Christmas and holidays all together," Molly told me, "so the children don't have to choose."

Helena, the Washington, DC, epidemiologist, told me about holidays at her house: "Currently, since my ex-husband Peter lives nearby, we're able to have holidays together, along with my current husband of seventeen years, and a variety of combined family and friends from a multitude of connections. Thanksgiving at our house is a very special event—usually not just my ex, but my husband's ex and her current husband attend. They all contribute delicious family recipes. The children—ours, his, hers—all benefit from our ability to create such a warm and fun holiday event on a regular basis. It's something that we all look forward to every year. Various other friends of ours or the children's also attend, and they no longer find it strange that there are so many unusual strands to our 'family.'"

Joel, the biologist in Idaho, told me how he and his ex-wife handled holidays and other family occasions when their child, Hannah, was a young girl. "Judy and I shared many holidays together, sometimes including our parents in the mix. When Judy and Hannah came to visit me, I would often invite my friends over to see them. Thus, they got to know my closest friends pretty well. Perhaps because of this, when I started dating my friend, Cathy, and bringing her with me on visits, Judy was very accommodating, and said she felt it was very healthy for Hannah to be around 'a couple.'

"Judy also remarried shortly after Cathy and I got married. We would go to Southern California to visit Hannah, and everyone would have meals and share other activities together. We all got along great. I recall one time after dinner at Judy's, Hannah ran off to play, leaving the four of us at the table. Since Hannah was the reason we were together, her absence made it seem a little strange, but I think we all felt it was okay."

Adair, the San Francisco writer, has maintained an undiminished sense of family that includes both her ex and her current husband. "This Christmas," she told me, "Jim, Bill, the kids, and I all went to Tahoe together."

Mimi told me, "Years after our divorce, when our son announced he was getting married by a justice of the peace, I called Paul on the phone and said, 'Jeff is getting married!' And we ran down to the courthouse. At Jewish events, or Thanksgiving, or whatever, we were always together. We were never without the children and all of us were together."

David and Susan, who lived together in the seventies in a marriagelike situation, have remained close through the years. They both live in Berkeley now with their respective spouses and children. "We share Thanksgiving and stuff," David told me. "Susan is the godparent of my second daughter."

"We do pretty much spend all our holidays

together," Sybil told me, speaking of herself, her ex-husband Jonathan, their daughter, Jenny, and Jonathan's lover, Bob. "We have spent Christmas together in the past, and Jonathan usually spends the night with us so that he can be there when Jenny wakes up. He's invited Jenny and me to go to southern France this summer with him and Bob."

Sybil is just getting to the point where she's thinking about dating other men. "I have a wonderful support group of friends—I wouldn't have been able to make it as a single parent without them! I've hardly used babysitters at all, because Jenny and I have so many friends that are willing to do that. And Bob babysits for Jenny a lot, too."

Through all the turmoil and disappointment, Sybil and Jonathan have kept their larger sense of family intact. "In '97," she told me, "all of Jonathan's family went to his sister's house for Thanksgiving. Jonathan and I were separated—he was out of the closet. We all rendezvous'd at his sister's house: the parents, the siblings, everybody. It went really well. There's one relative who's kind of—I don't know—having a hard time accepting Jonathan. But everyone else was great."

Miriam spoke to me about the continuing close sense of family between her and her ex-husband Jeremy, their son, Jason, and Lee, Miriam's husband of the past twenty years. "There was a period," she said, "after Jason had moved to the City, when the three of us met—Jeremy, Jason, and I. Jason wanted to know about how it all started and everything that happened. You know, kids come into our lives and they don't know our history. He wanted to know the history of us, of me and Jeremy. So we had these wonderful times when we just sat and talked about our life together in Tripp, South Dakota, and I told him how and why we got married, and all this stuff. He was in therapy then. His therapist's idea was, you've got your parents: ask them. He did, and we told him."

Olivia told me that she and her young son, Zachary, still spend Christmas with her family. "The only difference is that Mike doesn't go with us now. Mike has Zachary on Thanksgiving, and I have him on Christmas. At some point when Zachary says, 'I don't want to go to my grandmother's house, I want to stay here,' well, then, we'll decide something different." I asked Olivia whether she ever spends holidays with Mike and

Charlie, her new partner. "No," she told me. "We haven't gotten to that point. Not holidays." When I asked her whether that would be hard for them, she answered, "Oh, I think so. I mean, maybe if Mike had someone in his life, if he was with someone, it would be different. At some point down the road, I could see sharing that. Mike's very friendly, and he and Charlie know each other, but he doesn't want to double date or anything."

Family holidays are the payoff for Muriel, who worked so hard and gave so much to keep things amicable between herself and her ex-husband, Max. "We're all close," she told me. "Last Thanksgiving, everybody was here with me: Max and his wife and his son stayed with me. And Federico and Mariana and their baby stayed with our friends. And we had Thanksgiving together the whole weekend. It was a real family thing.

"Max and I have always done things together, because we both love Federico. Whenever Federico's here, if Max was in town, I'd say, 'Come over and have dinner!' We always did that. I always invited him for all the holidays—like Christmas, Thanksgiving, whatever. He was always part of any family celebration we had. Christmas is a family time for me, with my nieces, and two of my closest family friends who Federico grew up with—their daughter is like his sister."

Speaking of herself, her ex-husband Michael, and his wife Lara, Julie told me, "We've done a lot of Christmases together, a lot of Thanksgivings. We always celebrate birthdays together. If I'm having my birthday dinner with my family, Michael and Lara always join us. My dad is close to both of them. Sometimes just me and my dad and Lara go out! Lara loves my niece and nephew, and she always has presents for them. We really laugh a lot together, the three of us. Probably a disgusting amount! I don't laugh harder with anybody else than with these two, where I really can't control myself."

Both "family" and "village" are words that have a wide embrace. A parent and child, if closely bonded, make both a village and a family, in the narrowest senses of those words. Charles Dickens, in *Oliver Twist*, showed how a group of street urchins and their adult exploiter in nineteenth-century London made both a village and a family. We don't have to move out of the industrialized Western world—or the twenty-first century—to recapture what is best about both villages and families. We are surrounded by both, in our cities, in our suburbs, in our medium-sized and small towns. It's just that our focus has turned inward upon what is immediately ours—on the nuclear family, its material possessions, and property—that we've ceased to see what's before our eyes.

For Muriel, the village is populated by her friends and the needy people she serves, by her son and his wife and child, by her sister's children, and by her ex-husband and his wife and child. Dorian and Bianca, Molly and Noah, and the two children adored by all four of them are their own little village. Adair, her ex-husband Jim, their two children, and Adair's current husband, Bill, have made a little village in their two-household home in San Francisco.

Julie's village is largely populated by lithe, graceful people who wear tights a lot of the time and who love to laugh—although others, she hastens to add, are welcome.

For Olivia, the village is made of her son Zachary, her partner Charlie, Zachary's father, and Charlie's children by his first wife.

Joel's village is presided over by his wife Cathy,

and filled with the laughter of their two children and of Hannah, his daughter from his earlier marriage.

Miriam lives in a village that stretches from San Francisco Bay to the wine country, embracing her husband, Lee, her oldest best friend and ex-husband, Jeremy, their beloved son, Jason, and Lee's grown son from his first marriage.

Sybil's village is filled with her friends, presided over by her eight-year-old daughter Jenny, and graced with the part-time presence of Jenny's dad, Jonathan, and his lover, Bob.

Noël and Josie's village stretches over three continents, embracing their new partners, their children and a grandchild.

Helena and Peter's village is a half-hour drive from end to end but has a wide, rich sweep of extended family and friends.

Ellen's village reaches even beyond the world of the living, where it embraces her daughter Charlotte's eccentric and beloved late father, Ernie.

It takes a village to make a family. And it takes open eyes and a loving, forgiving heart to see the village and live inside its embrace.

CHAPTER SEVEN

Strange Bedfellows

"There aren't exactly rules for the kind of family we are. We are, I guess, the family of the 90s, the kind who go on vacation with their exes instead of pouring sugar down their gas tanks." — *Adair*

MOST PEOPLE WILL find the stories in this section to be rather amazing—and that's because it's still uncommon to hear of formerly married people choosing to spend leisure time together. If I could wave a magic wand and change the world—well, I would change a lot of things. But one of the many things I would change would be society's attitude about the intense compartmentalization of our lives: vacations are for nuclear families only, or for same-sex groups of friends. DNA tests or documentation as "official friend of family" are required for admission to significant holiday dinners. If you're "only" related by marriage—and a defunct marriage, at that—you can't have any of the turkey. If you're really old or really poor, you can't sit at our table unless you're related by blood—in which case, we'll tolerate you for finite amounts of time at designated periods of the year.

In short, I would make us a less exclusive, more inclusive nation of people, much more inclined than we are at present to share the love and abundance in our lives. I would also make life post-divorce much more inclusive than it is now, in tribute to the strong ties forged by marriage and the potential for warmth, cooperation, and fun that doesn't have to be scotched after the divorce papers are signed.

Peter, the epidemiologist, told me about the many ways that he and his ex-wife Helena have tapped into that potential. "It can involve dinners, holidays, shopping," he wrote to me, "mutual household help, support during times of illness. I attended Helena's wedding. I have stayed at her house with women I've been involved with. I occasionally seek her advice about important matters, including relationships."

Joel wrote to me, "When our daughter Hannah was young, Judy and I would take turns visiting each other every couple of months or so. We made this easy on each other's pocketbook by staying at the other's home (sleeping on the sofa, though!).

"Judy and I are both biologists and work in the same area of specialization. There is a big annual conference that we both attend. In the past, she would bring Hannah and her other child to the conference and have her parents watch the kids (her father also is a biologist in the same area of specialization—small world!). One year, because Judy's mother was recovering from surgery, her parents decided they could not attend the conference—so Judy was in need of childcare. The conference was being held a few hours' drive from our city, and my wife Cathy called Judy and offered to watch Hannah and Jessica. So, Judy flew to Idaho, left the kids with Cathy, and she, I, and a co-worker of mine went off to the conference. We got a lot of raised eyebrows on this—Cathy told people, 'Joel went to the conference with his ex-wife, and I'm watching her kids!'"

Joel went on, "The next summer, Cathy and I and our children took a two-week vacation in Southern California and Mexico. As usual, Hannah had been visiting us for a few weeks. We flew to

Mexico and stayed at the beach for a week before arriving at Judy's home, and then we stayed there for a week. The younger kids hit it off really well (I referred to them as 'quarter sisters' since they are all Hannah's half-sisters) and we all did a lot of fun things together. Before we came, Judy observed that Cathy's and my tenth anniversary would occur during our visit. She volunteered to watch all the kids so that Cathy and I could go away overnight to a B&B in Mendocino."

Colin, the British-born television producer, wrote to me, "My ex and I, who were divorced after twenty-two years of marriage and three children (now aged thirty-eight, thirty-seven and thirty-two), have remained on excellent terms since 1983. We spend time in each other's homes— I cook for her and her new husband, a very nice man. We spend the holidays in each other's homes and everyone is genuinely loving. She is the mother of my daughters and the grandmother of my granddaughters (four total so far). We have been able to supervise jointly the weddings of two of our three daughters."

Adair, the San Francisco writer, describes her own "strange bedfellows" situation with characteristic flair. "Since 1991, when my new husband Bill and I bought a flat from my ex-husband Jim in his building and moved in underneath him, we have all been like a family. We have dinner together on Sunday nights and sometimes more often. There aren't exactly rules for the kind of family we are. We are, I guess, the family of the 90s, the kind who go on vacation with their exes instead of pouring sugar down their gas tanks. There's a garden apartment downstairs that a friend suggests we should offer to Bill's ex-wife.

"We've been living like this since 1992," Adair continued, "and I suppose a shrink would say that our boundaries are becoming fluid. Jim sends bowls of soup, cake servers, and eggs downstairs, and stores his wine in our extra refrigerator. He comes down to show me funny things in the Clark, South Dakota newspaper, to use my fax machine, to ask me to read over something he's written for a book jacket, to discuss the state of the roof, to show us how to unstop the bathroom sink, or to demand that we make an immediate appointment with Patrick's social studies teacher.

"He walks in unannounced, always calling, 'Hello!' but then using his key. Sometimes Bill, imagining himself alone reading the paper in the early morning, is surprised to hear Jim in Patrick's bedroom arguing with him. I go upstairs to steal apples from Jim's kitchen (we call it the 'Jimstore' as in, 'We're out of rice. Can you get some up at the Jimstore?'). Kids who come over ring both our doorbells at once, just to see who comes to the door first. So does the UPS man, and, of course, at our door, the postman always rings twice.

"In a fit of housekeeping," Adair told me, "I once threw out a huge ball of unmated socks. 'Oh, I know you did,' Jim said when I mentioned it weeks later. 'I found it in the trash and took it upstairs. Turns out I had most of the mates.'

"There's a lot of traffic on the back stairs," Adair went on. "Jim came down and watched television with the cat while Bill and I were in Cape Cod this summer. This Saturday, when Bill overwatered his cactus pot, he sent Patrick upstairs to ask Jim for a turkey baster to drain the pot. Jim sent a message back with Patrick saying that if Bill was making turkey, he had some potatoes and green beans that would go well with it.

"It isn't an extended family exactly, but in another way it is. Jim came upon me in his kitchen, stealing a tomato, and instead of showing surprise, he started talking to me about the kids' homework. His brother-in-law materialized in my kitchen as I was making myself a solitary cup of tea."

Adair concluded, "My children, Morgan and Patrick, think it's one big house. I heard Morgan tell somebody on the phone, 'All of my parents are going out. Can't you come over?'"

Franny and Paul were married almost twenty years and had two children together. "Shortly after our divorce," she told me in a phone interview, "we were living in Miami, and my former husband decided he was going to move to California and take our son there just for a visit. And one of my friends said, 'Oh, he'll never send him back. You better go to California, too.' So I went with my daughter, and I couldn't afford to get an apartment." In Franny's East Coast diction, this sounded like "*a-pot-ment.*" "You talk about sharing—we shared an apartment for two years." This was after Franny and Paul were divorced. "Our children were twelve and fifteen. It was a two-bedroom: I shared my bedroom with our daughter, and he was with our son. It worked very nicely for me, and I guess for him, too. And then we were sort of on our own, and he moved downtown to San Diego. And so did I, because my son was in the Navy at the time.

"Paul talked me into moving into the same apartment building because it was less expensive for me. We were together every single day—whether we went walking or shopping. Every time I came downstairs in the elevator, this one particular man would say, 'Oh, your husband just went into the rec room.' And I'd say, 'He's not my husband.' 'Oh, yes he is, yes he is!' 'No, he's not!' They'd see us together all the time, and they couldn't believe that we were divorced."

Franny went on, "Paul lived on the thirteenth floor, I lived on the third floor, and the man I was dating at that time was on the seventh floor. So, I mean, it was a very funny situation. You know, we'd go to clubs together. And the man I was dating, he didn't like the idea that Paul was there. And I'd say, 'But we're divorced!' And he'd say, 'Well, you sure don't look like you are!'

"For two years, that other time, we shared an apartment." Franny started laughing at the memory. "This one was like an exclusive apartment, very pretty. The next door neighbors, who were about ten, fifteen years younger than we were, took a particular liking to me and Paul. We saw each other all the time, but we never volunteered to this couple that we were divorced. They had some sort of cabin on a lake, and they wanted us to come on vacation with them there; and we finally had to tell them that we were divorced—we couldn't go, because we're not sharing a bedroom. They couldn't believe it, because we get along so well, even now."

Paul, in his eighties now, lives in the Jewish Home for the Aged in San Francisco. Franny told me, "The man I've been going with now for four years drives me to San Francisco to see Paul. I can't see him that often, because there's no public transportation to get there, and it's about an hour's drive away. And my friend will say, 'I'll take you there once a month to visit Paul.' And I'll say, 'No, you've got to take me more often.'"

Olivia's ex-husband, Mike, lives right next door to her. "Together," she told me, "we bought five acres with two homes on it—one with a one-bedroom cottage. Just about the time we were separating, our tenants in the one-bedroom cottage moved out, so Mike just moved next door. We're literally on the same property, and our son goes in between.

"Mike can't live next door forever, even though he would if he could. It was supposed to be a transition thing for Zachary. We wanted the only blip in Zachary's screen to be that his dad was no longer sleeping in this house. We didn't want him to feel any other tremors. Our situations are pretty great, in those terms—you can't get any more ideal."

Muriel and Max have found themselves in many "strange bedfellows" situations over the years. "When Federico graduated from college," Muriel told me, "I went to the graduation and so did Max. We shared a cabin, because it was extremely hard to find anyplace at all to stay. We also went to Yosemite together when Federico was in high school. We stayed in a condo and went cross-country skiing together. That was a lovely time. We played Scrabble at night and had picnics."

Muriel continued, "At Federico's wedding, Max was there with his wife Jeanette, and I was there, of course, and it was a moving occasion for all of us. And more recently, Federico had them all at his house for the first time, over Christmas. He wanted

Max to have a wonderful time, and did everything to make it fun—bought a sled and went skiing, all these lovely things that they did together."

Julie recalled a time when she, her ex-husband Michael, and his wife Lara shared a hotel room. "The three of us went to a wedding together in Fresno last year," Julie told me. "We drove together and we stayed overnight in a nice hotel, and we shared one room to save on expenses. It was so funny, because first of all, Michael and Lara were sleeping in one bed and I was in the other bed. Lara had fallen asleep, and I was just drifting off, and Michael was working out. He exercises every night—sit-ups and push-ups. I was almost asleep when I saw him just look over. He looked at me in bed, and then he looked at Lara in the other bed, and he got this look on his face as if he was thinking, 'Oh, man, this is so weird!' Here were his two wives! And we both cracked up."

Bianca told me, "We spend most of our holidays and take our summer vacation at the beach all together. Noah and I take a walk or a drive together now and then, and he and Molly sometimes do me the honor of asking my advice when they are designing one of their remodeling projects. Molly and I are still best friends. I am very much in love with everyone in our family of six, and I have nothing but awe and gratitude for the transitions and transformations we all went through together, and for the fact that two dear children still remind us of our aim and potential to create a harmonious family. Life has not been monotonous, and all the crying has been well worth it!"

If you get beyond the pain, the anger, and the resentment (if you have any) of being left out of your ex-spouse's romantic future, the possibilities for friendship and fellowship between you are as great as those between any two devoted, lifelong friends. These possibilities have a broad range—anywhere from friendly, occasional phone calls to sharing vacations together with your extended families. (Few ex-spouses would want to go as far as Franny and Paul, who actually shared an apartment together!)

Unlike marriage, friendship is not at all narrowly defined. Even when the friends in question are ex-spouses, we are free to make up the rules as we go along, forging a friendship that meets our needs for continuity and connection.

CHAPTER EIGHT

Sex with Your Ex

*"**I**t was pleasurable, sure—but it didn't feel at all right. It was a way, maybe, of pretending for a few moments that what was so obviously happening in our marriage hadn't ever happened."* — *Samantha*

I WAS CURIOUS whether these highly amicable exes ever availed themselves of the opportunity to have sex with each other. After all, this was an aspect of the life they had shared together; it would probably feel familiar (if not necessarily comfortable). And being single after being partnered up for a long time can feel pretty lonely. I was somewhat surprised to learn that only one of the ex-couples among my interviewees had continued their intimate relationship after divorce.

Peter the epidemiologist told me, "We did not have that kind of closeness during our separation, and have not since the divorce in any way been physically close. I believe that interferes with the necessary emotional separation that determines whether people can truly move on."

Adair wrote, "We didn't go on having sex, but I did that once with an ex-boyfriend, who used to drop in on Saturdays when he was out running errands. It was frank, friendly, fun, and just ended after a few months."

For Susan and David, it wasn't altogether clear just when they became exes, since they kept splitting up and getting together again. "It's hard to say when we really broke up," she told me. "I think, like a lot of things, it kind of had fits and starts there."

When queried about the subject, Olivia said, "I think that's really very common with most people. Depending on the period of time or what's gone on, I think there's still some attraction there. I think most people have a tendency to forget the bad stuff. You only remember the good stuff. I've gotten to the point now where I look at Mike—I mean, I want to hug him, I want to hold him, I want to kiss him. I just want it all to be okay. I don't want to sleep with him. It actually goes back probably to more of a mothering kind of thing."

Nurturing, rather than ongoing intimacy, came up as a recurring theme as I spoke to people. Muriel told me, "After we were separated—we weren't divorced yet—Max moved out and I helped him. I said, 'All right, you need a blanket, you need some clothes, you need some food.' And he was moving in with a girlfriend! He's moving out, leaving me, and I'm supplying him with all these things. And I really wanted the marriage to keep going. We had gone to a counselor, and the guy talked to me afterwards, 'You know, both people have to want to make the marriage work. Obviously Max is not interested in the marriage working any more. So, let it go!' That was the last time we ever made love."

Julie told me emphatically, "We never have been together in that way since our separation. It was over when it was over. Definitely."

Joan and Ritch were the great exception. Joan told me that Ritch sometimes visits her in Kauai. "I also come to the Bay Area two times a year, and we always get together for a day and a night, at least when we both clear our schedules to be together. Inevitably we find other times during these trips to get together as well. We love to sleep together and wake up together. There is a place for me curled into his right side, held by his right arm that is like no other.

"Sexually, we have gone through many different spaces. Over the years, this has been a source of both pleasure and emotional pain. Most recently I decided I did not want to be sexual with Ritch. But this is always open to life's unfolding: to be open to continuing our sexual relationship—and being free to say no to that when either of us needed to."

Ritch told me, "Sex has continued to be a part of our relationship. Because in our marriage some of the issues that came up between us were sexual, that still shows up sometimes. Each time Joan and I get together, we don't assume that we'll be sexual together. But it's always a possibility. And we just pay attention to what feels right in the moment." The two meet at least once a year, on their wedding anniversary. "When we got together that next May after we separated, Joan had said something like, 'No matter where we are, let's make sure we get together every year on our anniversary.' I remember thinking, 'All things considered, that's a really great idea—and I'm not sure I can commit to that! Who knows where we'll be, or how that will work when we're in relationship with someone else?' But we have, actually—I think there's only been two years, maybe three, when we have not been physically together. I remember one year I was up at a resort spot in Calistoga with some friends. We set up a phone call, and I was on the phone with Joan for an hour. But, typically, either I'm going to see her there, or she's coming here."

When I asked Ritch whether the infatuation ever ended between him and Joan, he heaved a big sigh. "I don't know if I'd call it infatuation. But right now she's still the love of my life. I think I have the space and the capacity to invite somebody else in, in that way. I know I have the desire. Anyone I get involved with knows about Joan pretty much from the start. We're both clear that anyone we get involved with has to accept the other in our life—maybe not sexually. That's the part that would be okay to let go of. But if my new mate, beloved, doesn't accept Joan and her place in my life, then on some level, she's just not right for me. She doesn't have to become friends with Joan—although it would be great if they liked each other. But she has to accept and honor my relationship with Joan. I hope that this new person will become the love of my life. But so far, I still have great love for Joan, and I know she has for me, too."

Samantha wrote to me, "There was a period of about four months when Jake was still living in the house with me and our daughter, but we knew our marriage was ending and he was sleeping on the couch. Our daughter was always trying to lure us both into the same bed with her to cuddle. It felt very sad to me. In some ways, both Jake and I wanted what she wanted—just to be there for each other in a familiar, comforting way.

"I think there were two different nights during that time when I invited Jake into bed with me, after Lily was asleep in her room. I was lonely; and Jake seemed so needy. But it was just too confusing for all of us, especially when Lily came into our room one morning and found us there together. It was pleasurable, sure—but it didn't feel at all right. It was a way, maybe, of pretending for a few moments that what was so obviously happening in our marriage hadn't ever happened. Both of us had wanted very much for our marriage to last; and we both did everything we were capable of doing at that time to work things out, to find a way. But we really were past the point of no return then.

"When Jake moved out into his own place," Samantha continued, "that was it. We've never been intimate again, and I can't even imagine it now. It would seem—I don't know—incestuous. Jake feels to me now like a wonderful and cherished member of my extended family."

Obviously, in this highly charged and highly tricky area, every couple must find their own way. But it does seem that Peter's comment reflects what most of these couples have come to believe: sex with your ex only muddies the boundaries and makes it hard to move on.

CHAPTER NINE

A New Vision of Both Yourself and the Person You Married

*"**I** don't imagine that this acceptance could work if we were still a married couple. But, as an ex, it's easier to see that Peter is simply a human being with a whole range of complicated attributes, some difficult—especially for me—and some very wonderful."* — *Helena*

IT IS VERY hard to see either yourself or another person clearly and honestly, without the filters imposed by prejudice, personal history, and hope. One of the things that emerged from my interviews was a certain clarity of vision among the amicable exes I spoke with. I touched on this in Chapter Two. It does seem that insight is the final stage in the journey from divorce to amicability.

Of course, you don't see everything in your life clearly just because you've reached a state of reconciliation with your ex-spouse; there's always a lot left to learn. But there seems to be a particularly unfiltered view of the marital and post-marital relationship that is visited on those who have gone through the five stages, from anger to insight.

I remember when my mother's cousin Albert was dying but still able to speak. I hung on his every word, feeling that what he said in these final moments would be truthful in every way. There's a similar sense of truthfulness in the way the people in this book were able to speak about themselves in relationship to their ex, a certain startling clarity in their view of their ex. With distance from their marriage, and in the undisturbed atmosphere of acceptance, they seemed capable of simply observing themselves and one another without reacting emotionally to what they saw. They were able to observe without an agenda, perhaps in much the same way that dying people can look at and comment on life.

When we're in love, we don't at all see clearly. When we're in the throes of disappointment, hurt, and anger, we don't see clearly either. We may convince ourselves that we are seeing with perfect clarity in both states of being. But both are fraught with equally powerful distortions. In love, we make things more wonderful, more ideal than they really are. We gloss or gild over anything that displeases us. In anger, hurt, or hate, we only see and hear the qualities and behaviors that are driving us crazy. Equipped with cruelly distorting glasses, we become incapable of seeing those qualities and behaviors in the once-loved one that may still be beautiful, admirable, or endearing.

In amicability, though, I truly believe that we approach twenty-twenty emotional vision. We see the person we loved. We see the person we very consciously chose not to be married to anymore (or who chose not to be married to us anymore). The reasons we're ultimately incompatible shine just as clearly as the reasons why we were drawn together in the first place. We see each other, more or less, without judgment. There is sufficient distance between us to prevent the pressing of one another's buttons.

Peter, the epidemiologist, told me, "After the divorce was the first time that I got enough distance to see Helena as a human being and not just an extension of my needs and feelings. Significant illness was a big factor in the deepening of love and appreciation of separateness—for me with her. I still find her somewhat rough-edged and very controlling. I just don't get caught in it anymore, and I don't depend on her affections for my survival."

I asked Peter if there are some qualities in Helena that make him particularly grateful that she's the other parent of their child. "Mostly just how fantastically bright she is—that has transferred to our son. I'd also add her great love of family, which is something we share."

Helena told me, "I would say that Peter is a wonderfully sensitive and caring human being. As a friend, he has a great ability to listen and give his undivided attention. He is attuned to many levels of the conversation and can often give useful advice and feedback.

"I don't imagine," continued Helena, "that this acceptance could work if we were still a married couple. But, as an ex, it's easier to see that Peter is simply a human being with a whole range of complicated attributes, some difficult—especially for me—and some very wonderful."

Colin, the television producer, said of his ex-wife, "She is among the most decent, loving, kind and considerate people I have ever known. Her efforts on behalf of our kids, from infancy on, were unstinting and often deeply self-sacrificial. She has passed to our daughters a role model and a legacy of quality and integrity that will help them for life."

Joan wrote to me from Kauai, "Ritch has a very pure heart. He loves me more unconditionally than anyone else ever has—apart from my father. And it has been Ritch's love that has helped me to be able to recognize and receive my father's love. Ritch is my teacher in unconditional love. I have a clarity of mind and a persistent commitment to the truth that teaches him to dive deeper into himself. I bring mind to his heart and he brings heart to my mind."

For his part, Ritch told me, "I saw myself more clearly after the separation. I had to really look at my part in what didn't work, and somehow I was able to look at it better when I was out of the relationship. At that point, I could accept some of the things she had been telling me all along. And there were other things where I said, 'No, I think this is your stuff here.' I saw some parts of Joan more clearly, but more than this, I could see myself more clearly."

Muriel seems to be very clear about the man to whom she's been emotionally tied, inside and outside of marriage, for most of her adult life. "Max is very dogmatic," she told me. "Whenever I see him, I realize that I'm glad I'm not married to him anymore. He's brilliant and powerful—and he's difficult to live with!"

I asked Muriel, who is an accomplished, internationally exhibited painter, whether she feels that Max, a world-renown conductor, has sufficiently honored her artistic gift while fulfilling his own. She answered a little tentatively. "I think he did much more after we were divorced. He'd be very proud of the things I was doing; and he'd always have suggestions, 'Oh, you should do this and that!' He always told me he was proud. But it was a conflict for him while we were married."

Julie spoke about her post-divorce view of Michael, her ex-husband and ballet partner—and I thought about Muriel and Max's situation, about two people in the arts trying to be married to each other. In the successful artist couples I've known, one member of the pair usually shines more brightly than the other; they function like the sun and the moon, one burning hard, the other reflecting brilliantly. "Michael is a very creative person," Julie told me. "He probably exemplifies the definition of the word 'artist' more than any other person I know. He makes things work so that he can pursue his art. He wants to do his art."

I asked Julie about the dynamics of their partnership, both on and off the stage. Julie replied, "Michael knows a lot and he likes to be a coach. He grew up in sports, he played a lot of football; he was a great athlete. He's a teacher. He has great ideas. A lot of what happened with us when we were a young couple was that when I finally found my voice—when I arrived at a level professionally where I was competent—it changed the dynamic a little bit between us. I felt that he wasn't giving me room to have my voice. I felt like he still wanted to be in charge of this couple. And it took some adjustment to even it out until we reached that place eventually where we both had equal input." Julie and Michael only fully occupied this place after their divorce.

"I think that Michael sometimes has a hard time finding the words to express what he's really feeling, but he knows what he's feeling. So a lot of times, I'll give him the words. And he'll say, 'Yeah!

That's what I mean.' And Lara does that, too, because she's very articulate, and she does that for him as well. But Michael can convey anything through his body," Julie told me, "through dance.

"What happens with dance—and maybe this is a metaphor for relationship—is that you get to a point, especially when you're working with a partner, where you've worked on your technique for so many years, you've disciplined yourself to obey certain rules that become so natural, that at a certain point you don't have to think about them anymore. We've rehearsed so much that we're not thinking about what to do next. We're able to go into this new space of not knowing what's going to happen. And everything works. It becomes spontaneous, and different things emerge each time."

Julie's descriptions of the dance experience really do provide an apt metaphor for the marital bond. She went on, "When we were dancing, nothing felt better than the two of us moving at the same time, because it didn't feel like two of us. It felt like one of us. The pattern of a *pas de deux* mirrors what happens in a relationship. You start out together. Everything feels perfectly synchronized, and you're supporting your partner the whole way through. And then each partner has to perform a solo alone on the stage, and the other partner is always standing in the wings, watching, rooting for the other person. You're sending them all your good energy to do well, but there's really nothing you can do to help them. They're on their own. And you get really upset if they mess up, because you know how they're going to feel. And that kind of models a relationship, too, because you're not always doing everything together, and you want to be supportive of your partner's individual endeavors and give them space to do their own thing. But you always come back together at the end for the coda, the finale."

Julie has obviously spent years thinking about all of this and processing her observations. She is full of life and promise, and seems very ready to welcome the new relationships that await her. She also strikes one as amazingly humble, both in her assessment of the work she's done and her expectations for the future.

"I really have to say," she told me, "that even after everything I've been through, I still don't fully understand what it is that makes relationships work. But I do know that whatever happens,

Michael and Lara and I are always going to be friends."

Life after divorce is no more static than is life at any other stage. The lens through which you view both yourself and your ex-spouse may require adjustment from time to time. Images and insights may go in and out of focus. The people within your field of vision will change. You will no doubt revise many of your opinions as time goes on, because this is what normally happens as people grow older.

CHAPTER TEN

Growing Old Together Anyway

*"**P**aul's older daughter, the one from the first marriage, used to say to me, 'When are you and Dad going to separate?' We were divorced but not separated. I would say, 'I don't know. Probably never.' And I used to say to Paul, 'We always said we'd grow old together. Little did we know that we are growing old together.'"*
— *Franny*

THERE ARE A lot of sentimental—and beautiful—songs about married people growing old together. While most couples in the first flush of youth don't obsess overmuch about the prospect of their gray hairs mingling on the pillowcase someday, every married couple has probably given at least a passing thought to the idea of becoming a terribly sweet and affectionate pair of old folks. Certainly the prospect of growing old side by side with a beloved mate is much more palatable than the prospect of growing old all alone.

Losing the dream of affectionate, daily companionship into old age is one of the bitterest pills to swallow in the handful of bitter pills offered us by divorce. It's hard enough feeling one's own physical and mental capacities diminish as the decades fly by. But to face the results of time and gravity without anyone by your side who remembers you when you were a hot number—this must be very dismal indeed.

I firmly believe that one is never too old to experience romantic passion. My mom, in her late sixties, had a wild, wonderful love affair for two of the happiest years of her life with a man who was over seventy. And I know that life would be a lot better for her now if he were still alive.

My mom's case is somewhat unusual. Usually it is the companions of our youth and middle age who keep our spirits young, because we are as young in their eyes as we are in our own.

One of the great side benefits of having an amicable relationship with your ex-spouse is that you get to grow old together anyway. People who divorce with rancor and lose touch with each

other find that whole eras of their life are pre-
served, at best, in their own memories only. At
worst, whole eras, out of the individual's bitterness
and distaste for the memories they hold, are consigned to the compost pile. But then we lose everything good along with everything that was bad.

I won't belabor the point, but I think there is
common consensus about the excellent value to be
found in old friends. Your ex-spouse, if currently
part of your circle of extended family and friends,
is a walking scrapbook of memories, a testimonial
to your youthful charms and follies, and a camera
that will take decades off you more astonishingly
than a Beverly Hills facelift.

Being amicable ex-spouses is a variation of having your cake and eating it, too.

Adair told me, "Jim and I are still raising the
kids together, going together to confront deans
and teachers, conferring on a daily basis on decisions regarding the two kids. As Bill will tell you,
Jim and I agree on child-raising matters because
we're both such pushovers.

"Going up to Jim's flat is always, fleetingly, like
stepping into my own past. Jim never changes anything. The pictures on the walls are all of the kids

when they were under five, because I put them there. My hats are in the downstairs closet, my baby albums on the living room shelves, my college texts in the attic, my old coats in boxes upstairs, my former husband reading the paper at the kitchen table."

Franny has known her ex-husband Paul for over forty years. "At the point when Paul got sick," Franny told me, "he had four children, two from another marriage. And I was the one who decided, well, he's gonna come live with me. I'll take care of him. So I tried, but I couldn't. I thought I was Mother Theresa, but I'm not. But, anyway, we remained friends, and I went to visit him every single day. You talk about devotion—that's what we have. We got along better after our divorce, because the things that annoyed me I could care less about now, because we weren't married—if that makes any sense.

"He had a cerebral aneurysm about three years ago, and then he had a stroke. Now he's in the Jewish Home for the Aged in San Francisco. I see him as often as I can get a ride from San Mateo. Paul's always very happy to see me, and everybody knows me there: 'Oh, you're Paul's wife.' 'No, I'm

Paul's ex-wife.' This is the way it's always been. I've always been very concerned about Paul. Any time his health is bad, my daughter would tell me and I'd get all excited. 'Oh,' she says, 'you're more upset about it than I am.'"

Franny continued, "Paul's older daughter, the one from the first marriage, used to say to me, 'When are you and Dad going to separate?' We were divorced but not separated. I would say, 'I don't know. Probably never.' And I used to say to Paul, 'We always said we'd grow old together. Little did we know that we *are* growing old together.'

"He's got four children, but I was the one that was most attentive to him. I'm not saying they're not good children, but they work, and I'm retired now. So they couldn't go to see him as often as I could. I was the one who was always there. My best days are when I'm with Paul. I mean, I'm very happy to see him."

Jeremy, Miriam, and their grown son, Jason, all met me for lunch at one of the fantastic houses on a hill in San Francisco that sports several of Jeremy's architectural designs. Jeremy's partner wandered in at one point to greet us. Jeremy and Miriam were poring over yearbooks and privately published histories of their hometown in South Dakota. One could almost hear the whoosh of the passage of time, looking from the school pictures of the two to the two of them as they are today— a loving, eternally bonded pair of ex-spouses. After I left them to walk to my car, I turned around for a moment and watched them say their own good-byes, clinched in an enormous bear hug.

For Ritch and Joan, marriage and divorce entailed lifelong pair-bonding in a realm that supercedes geographical proximity. Joan wrote to me from Kauai, "Ritch had our wedding rings inscribed 'Ritch and Joan forever'—and that pretty much describes this connection we have."

Ritch told me, "When we used to sign cards, we had these interconnected hearts that read, 'JL and RD forever.' And I still believe that. It's just not about being physically together or married physically forever, but we are in each other's lives forever."

David and Susan, who were live-in lovers during and after college, definitely keep each other's youth alive. "One of the very nice things about my new house," Susan confided to me, "is that it's so close to David's—just two blocks away!" Happily married to other people, the two are watching their children grow up together and are clearly oblivious to the ravages of time. David sees Susan as a freckle-faced flower-child; Susan sees David as a slender youth with drooping mustaches and abundant long hair.

Sybil couldn't possibly have anticipated the turn of events that ended her marriage to Jonathan, who had a reputation in high school as a ladies' man. They both entered into marriage with every intention of an enduring marital bond. Things just didn't work out that way. Jonathan's walk out of the closet was as much a surprise to him, apparently, as it was to Sybil. As a young bride Sybil would have been very surprised to glimpse her future that would contain both Jonathan and his lover, Bob. "I did get married with the idea," Sybil told me over the telephone, "that we would grow old together." I could hear the wistful smile in her voice as she said, "And we will, just in a different way."

Julie has reserved a park bench big enough to hold her, Michael, and Michael's wife, Lara—with some room left over for one more adult of the male persuasion and wiggle room for any little ones who may burst onto the scene. She's not about to miss out on the fun of growing old together with one of her favorite people on earth. "Michael's someone in my life who's a staple, who will always be in my life. I just know we'll share certain things that we won't share with other people. One of the nice things, too, is that I know Michael feels I understand him in a way no one else does, because of our long history together and growing up together, really. Sometimes when he calls me and says certain things, I have the feeling he just needs to know in that moment that I know how he really is and who he really is."

Julie flashed one of her brilliant smiles. "I know we're going to be laughing together when we're eighty, if we're still alive!"

As Julie and all the others have shown, building a friendship out of the ruins of a marriage is never easy. But what a gift such friendships are to all involved: the ex-spouses, their children, their extended families, and even generations to come.

We may have to travel over a rough, treacherous road before reaching the place where we can say, "We're divorced now, but we're still friends." But for all the ex-spouses who can say this and feel it in their hearts, the pleasures of the destination merit every difficulty encountered along the way.

Endnotes

Chapter 1: A Consideration of Marriage

1. Kirsten Olsen, *Chronology of Women's History* (Westport, CN: Greenwood Publishing Group, 1994), 136.

2. John Mordechi Gottman, *The Seven Principles to Making Marriage Work* (NY: Crown Publishing Group, Inc., 1999).

3. Rita Rudner, "Born To Be Mild," 1990.

Chapter 2: Navigating the Rocky Road

1. Daphne Rose Kingma, *Coming Apart: Why Relationships End and How to Live Through the Ending of Yours* (Berkeley, CA: Conari Press, 1987), 16.

2. Ibid., xii.

Acknowledgments

I would like to thank my parents, Edie and Hal, who both, in their separate ways, taught me to hang on tight to my sense of humor. I owe a debt of warmth, love, and gratitude to my mother outlaw, Gay, who has reacted to the tedious stream of manuscript drafts with unflagging enthusiasm and encouragement. Likewise with George, who daily schools me in the arts of generosity, optimism, and *joie de vivre*. My dance teachers—Conceição, Georgia, and Bridget—kept my brain oxygenated, my heart open, and my feet in contact with the ground, making it possible to put in the requisite long hours at my computer. Belatedly, thanks and love in the same vein to Marina. The amicable exes who gave so generously of their stories and insights are, of course, the real authors of this book—for without the trails they blazed, it could never have been written.

About the Author

A regular reviewer for the *New York Times Book Review* since 1984, Barbara Quick is the author of *Northern Edge: A Novel of Survival in Alaska's Arctic*. She has lectured, led seminars, and given keynote addresses at a number of universities, libraries, and writer's conferences, including UC Berkeley, UC Santa Cruz, UC Irvine, the University of Alaska at Fairbanks, California State University at Long Beach, and Prescott College in Arizona. *Northern Edge* has been part of the women's literature curriculum at several colleges and universities. Barbara's reviews, essays, and articles have appeared in *Newsweek*, *Ms.*, the *Los Angeles Times* and the *San Francisco Chronicle*; she has written under assignment for *People* magazine and *Cosmopolitan*. Barbara has some fifteen years of experience as a freelance editor and ghostwriter. She lives in Kensington, California, with her son Julian.

About the Press

Wildcat Canyon Press publishes books that embrace such subjects as friendship, spirituality, women's issues, and home and family, all with a focus on self-help and personal growth. Great care is taken to create books that inspire reflection and improve the quality of our lives. Our books invite sharing and are frequently given as gifts.

For a catalog of our publications, please write:

Wildcat Canyon Press
2716 Ninth Street
Berkeley, California 94710
Phone: (510) 848-3600
Fax: (510) 848-1326
or review our website at:
www.wildcatcanyon.com

More Wildcat Canyon Titles

I WAS MY MOTHER'S BRIDESMAID: YOUNG ADULTS
TALK ABOUT THRIVING IN A BLENDED FAMILY
The truth about growing up in a "combined family."
Erica Carlisle and Vanessa Carlisle
$13.95 ISBN 1-885171-34-X

THE COURAGE TO BE A STEPMOM: FINDING YOUR
PLACE WITHOUT LOSING YOURSELF
Hands-on advice and emotional support for
stepmothers.
Sue Patton Thoele
$14.95 ISBN 1-885171-28-5

CELEBRATING FAMILY: OUR LIFELONG BONDS WITH
PARENTS AND SIBLINGS
True stories about how baby boomers have recognized
the flaws of their families and come to love them as
they are.
Lisa Braver Moss
$13.95 ISBN 1-885171-30-7

AUNTIES: OUR OLDER, COOLER, WISER FRIENDS
An affectionate tribute to the unique and wonderful
women we call "Auntie."
Tamara Traeder and Julienne Bennett
$12.95 ISBN 1-885171-22-6

LITTLE SISTERS: THE LAST BUT NOT THE LEAST
A feisty look at the trials and tribulations, joys, and
advantages of being a little sister.
Carolyn Lieberg
$13.95 ISBN 1-885171-24-2

girlfriends: INVISIBLE BONDS, ENDURING TIES
Filled with true stories of ordinary women and
extraordinary friendships, *girlfriends* has become a
gift of love among women everywhere.
Carmen Renee Berry and Tamara Traeder
$12.95 ISBN 1-885171-08-0
Also Available: Hardcover gift edition, $20.00 ISBN
1-885171-20-X

girlfriends TALK ABOUT MEN: SHARING SECRETS FOR
A GREAT RELATIONSHIP
This book shares insights from real women in real
relationships—not just from the "experts."
Carmen Renee Berry and Tamara Traeder
$14.95 ISBN 1-885171-21-8

girlfriends FOR LIFE: FRIENDSHIPS WORTH
KEEPING FOREVER
This follow-up to the best-selling *girlfriends* is an
all-new collection of stories and anecdotes about the
amazing bonds of women's friendships.
Carmen Renee Berry and Tamara Traeder
$13.95 ISBN 1-885171-32-3

A COUPLE OF FRIENDS: THE REMARKABLE FRIENDSHIP
BETWEEN STRAIGHT WOMEN AND GAY MEN
What makes the friendships between straight women
and gay men so wonderful? Find out in this honest and
fascinating book.
Robert H. Hopcke and Laura Rafaty
$14.95 ISBN 1-885171-33-1

INDEPENDENT WOMEN: CREATING OUR LIVES, LIVING
OUR VISIONS
How women value independence and relationship and
are redefining their lives to accommodate both.
Debra Sands Miller
$16.95 ISBN 1-885171-25-0

THOSE WHO CAN...TEACH! CELEBRATING TEACHERS
WHO MAKE A DIFFERENCE
A tribute to our nation's teachers!
Lorraine Glennon and Mary Mohler
$12.95 ISBN 1-885171-35-8

THE WORRYWART'S COMPANION: TWENTY-ONE WAYS
TO SOOTHE YOURSELF AND WORRY SMART
The perfect gift for anyone who lies awake at night
worrying.
Dr. Beverly Potter
$11.95 ISBN 1-885171-15-3

Books are available at fine retailers nationwide.
Prices subject to change without notice.